Passion as Big as a Planet: Evolving Eco-Activism in America

Ma'ikwe Schaub Ludwig

Published by Ma'ikwe Schaub Ludwig

Zialua Ecovillage

Albuquerque NM

maikwe@solspace.net

(505) 514-8180

www.SolSpace.net

Cover art and design, and chapter art by Elizabeth Perrachione.

Passion is dedicated to:

My dedicated, intelligent, workhorse role model who also happens to be my dad, Dr. James Ludwig,

For inspiration from my childhood

The amazing, creative, joyful women I've come to think of as my "Triple Goddess of Albuquerque": Zaida Amaral, Chery Klairwator and Elizabeth Perrachione,

For inspiration in my day-to-day

And for my son, Jibran Walker Ludwig, and my birth daughter, Ananda Maya Amaral-Doyon, both of whom can create miracles when they put their minds and hearts to it,

For inspiration that will outlive me

Across three generations, you six
embody my best hopes for the world.
I love you.

Table of Contents:

Acknowledgments

First and foremost, I thank my parents for their primal contribution to this work: in addition to a body, they provided the basic stuff of a good childhood. In addition, my mom, Kay Howard, has been my biggest support person over the years, and my dad, Dr. James Ludwig, an inspiration for my life's work. Also, my brother Mark and his wife Kim are friends as well as family.

This work would never have come about if it wasn't for the Avatar®[1] Course. Harry Palmer has my deepest respect and gratitude for developing these tools. Both the content of this book and my own ability to get the thing written have deep roots in Avatar (though my words shouldn't be confused with a representation of the course; each one of us who do Avatar take it into our own lives in our own way). I can hardly imagine who I would be had I never discovered Avatar, though I'm certain I'd be insufferable; it's been that profound for me. In addition to Harry, I am indebted to the staff of Star's Edge, and the network of masters who are both companions and role models in our shared goal of creating a planet of peace, connection and sanity. Thank you.

The Intentional Communities Movement has held me over the years in a thousand ways; perhaps the most profound is giving me a sense of life-purpose, and a knowing that it is possible to put our lives together however we choose to... with friends! Thanks to the members of my communities: the Minis Kitigan Drum, East Wind, Sarvis Point, October Sky, Dancing Rabbit Ecovillage, Sol Space, Sandhill Farm and the Zialua Ecovillage (aka Home). Thanks as well

---

[1] Avatar is a registered trademark of Star's Edge, Inc. All rights reserved.

to all my companions at the Fellowship for Intentional Community, especially Tony Sirna, Alyson Ewald, Jenny Upton, Harvey Baker, Susan Patrice and Laird Schaub; to have beings just as committed as I am to fanning the flames of community is a tremendous gift.

My Albuquerque friends are the heart of my life, community and activism. In addition to being my best friends, Chery Klairwator, Zaida Amaral and Elizabeth Perrachione all supported this project with a combination of love, humor and butt-kickings as needed; I literally could not have done this without you. Jibran Ludwig, Marqis Rotenberg, Alberto Lopez, Ananda Amaral-Doyon, Denis Doyon, Christian Meuli, Steven Jackson, Loralee Makela, Michael Hyde, Victoria Lattanza, Kimi Foree, Rev Terrell, Almut Zieher, Kendra Toth, Chris Burbridge, Mary Lou Singleton, Melanie Rubin, Ima Mueller, Maggie Seeley and Rich Bowditch (and numerous others I'm undoubtedly neglecting to mention) all deserve acknowledgment for their various and sundry support roles, but mostly for just being the people I relax with, with absolute certainty that I am loved.

Deciding to write a book is one thing; having the tangible support from the universe to get it done is quite another! Bill Perry provided financial support to help make this possible in the context of a busy life. Thanks.

Thanks to Kay Howard, Laird Schaub and Robert Griffin for their comments on the book. Thanks to Darren Perrachione, Alberto Lopez, Hansa-Pria Pomeraning, Zaida Amaral and Chery Klairwator for participating in a cool little kinesiology experiment with the book that helped me cut to the chase on the final edits, and gave me a good dose of non-rational input. And thanks, a few hundred times over, to Elizabeth Perrachione, my editor, hand-holder and artist; your faith in this project from the beginning has been the single biggest factor (beyond my own determination) in this book getting out into the world! This book is so much better for all of your input.

I would be remiss if I didn't thank planet earth, particularly Lakes Michigan and Superior, and the Sandia Mountains for being my main loves of the physical planet. And for God, Goddess and the spirit of Wolf… thank you for holding me through my life with such care and guiding me toward a life of Service.

ii

Finally, my husband, Laird Schaub, is my rock. He is the partner who meets my heart, my vision and my passion like no one else. I love you, I am deeply grateful for you, and I am honored to be the woman you've chosen to share your life with.

I hope that each of you can see your little piece on these pages—this is truly a work of Community.

Ma'ikwe Schaub Ludwig
Albuquerque NM
April 2007

Passion as Big as a Planet:

Evolving Eco-Activism in America

By Ma'ikwe Schaub Ludwig

Introduction: Toward a Spiritual Activism

This is my home,
this is my only home.
This is the only sacred ground
I have ever known.
And should I stray
in the dark night alone,
rock me goddess
in the gentle arms of Eden.

--Dave Carter and Tracy Grammar, Gentle Arms of Eden

This is a book about something I call "enlightened activism." It is a blend of the two arenas I have spent the most time in during my life, both professional and personal: sustainability advocacy and personal growth. One of my own primary struggles in life has been how to have these two things co-exist peacefully within myself, how to blend the outwardly focused work called activism, with the inwardly focused work of spirituality. I have come to see that the microcosm of my own exploration and growth has a parallel track in the macrocosm of the world at large. At both levels, activism and spirituality complement and complete each other.

If activism is the outward thrust into the world of values for a better life, then spiritual growth is the inward drive to fully explore and develop those values, to ground them in compassion and integrity. You can't truly have one without the other, and expect it to be sustainable. In activism, we test our spiritual mettle in the greater world and allow it to affect others. We make it real for someone other than ourselves, and we get to see if those things we embrace as our spiritual truth are actually true anywhere other than our own minds and hearts. In the spiritual, we contemplate what is valuable and how we can best nurture and preserve it, and we can test it out in the domain where we can be fully present and free to develop and explore, without the cares and complications of the outer world intruding.

It is when we bring our spirituality and activism together that we create a sacred marriage that allows each to be fulfilled. Values without action are simply philosophy or self-indulgence. Action without values is empty and doomed to fail, if only in the long run when we can see that they were not grounded enough to survive the test of the world. Values and action; spirituality and activism.

To put it more succinctly: In our spirituality, we discover what is worth showing up for. In our activism, we show up.

There is also the side of the equation of what we get out of each of these (and here, too, is an important balancing act—the give and the take). Spiritual growth gives us a foundation to stand on. In a recent period of major change and loss, I found myself waking up each day with the deepest of gratitude for my spiritual work, because it has given me resiliency. On the other side, it is our activism—acting on our values, and achieving something both concrete and meaningful—that gives us the satisfaction of work well done. Activism is confidence building in a way that spiritual work alone never quite is, because our spiritual work can be invisible (even to ourselves at times) where achievements in the world are concrete.

We can protect our spiritual work, hide it and keep it safe and tender, locked into the narrow confines of our own immediate world. It is, after all, a vulnerable thing to share and even more vulnerable on which to act. But things cocooned tend to wither and die; certainly they don't flourish. We must take our spirituality out of the quiet of our personal lives, and put it into action. In this way, we create a spiritual life of real vibrancy.

By the same token, we can get locked into a one-track activism that never pauses for reflection. When we do this, we find ourselves seemingly fighting the same battle over and over again, with very little progress or joy. In this mode, essential questions about things like integrity get lost in the shuffle of needing to be right and win an argument. Both domains need the cross-fertilization of the other. Spirituality and activism each provide the way out of the other's most seductive traps.

Building a bridge between these two things is ultimately what

3

life is about.

So, why write a book focusing specifically on eco-activism? Partially, it is because this is what I know best. But there is also a more profound reason: For me, there is something particularly compelling about an activism that is tied directly to the ground I walk upon every day. The planet is the context for everything I do, regardless of whether I think my actions, hopes and dreams are related to the earth.

I believe that our relationship with the planet is a profoundly personal one—one that is at the heart of every dream we have ever dreamed, every opportunity we have ever been presented with, every last shred of what it means to be human. To be connected with a planet is both a profoundly spiritual thing, and the most mundane background noise in our lives. We live our lives, and we do it on the earth. We have bodies, and they are earth-bound bodies, composed of the very stuff of the earth around us, spun into a form we arbitrarily and temporarily label human. We dream, and we dream on the earth. We manifest dreams, and they spring from the earth. Being on a planet means having *opportunity* in the broadest, simplest and most profound sense.

This book is an exploration of opportunity, and in that way, it is a departure from typical environmentalism that puts the focus on the planet as both *limited and limiting*. This is the Left Wing's version of Armageddon: if we don't buy into this idea of limitation, and start behaving accordingly, we are all going to die. And in this process of creating our own deaths, we may be simultaneously participating in the heinous and unforgivable act of taking all life on the planet with us. Perhaps (in the most extreme scenario) we may succeed in removing from this planet its very ability to support life at all.

Sound depressingly familiar? This focus on limitation invites the impending gloom and doom that is inevitably and desperately associated with anything limited and being consumed. This focus is core to the recent history of the environmental movement. It is a belief that puts a tremendous amount of attention on what's wrong: wrong with us, wrong with our ways of living, and wrong with being human at all.

Perhaps this seems too extreme or too black and white, and it is possible that it is. But please bear with me. What I am addressing here is not so much about "truth" in some absolute way, but rather a general trend that is getting stronger as we move toward the various versions of doomsday that myself and other environmentalists have been claiming as the inevitable outcome of our current trajectory for many, many years.

And, yes, I count myself in that category. I am a third generation thinker along these lines. Up until a few years ago, doomsday thinking was a cornerstone of my sustainability work. This belief in the limited nature of being and what I style as "doomsday" thinking is as real for modern environmentalists as Armageddon is for true believers of that doctrine; I am going to challenge this however, because I believe that the implications of buying it hook, line and sinker are disastrous for us as a people.

Having said that, I have no wish to empower the perspective

that says the environmental movement is a bunch of alarmists and the relationship we have to the planet (and the abusive consciousness that runs through that relationship) is just fine. Denial is a perspective that says we ought not look too closely into our own consciousness or cultural practices. It is one path away from personal and cultural responsibility, and though my words could be — if taken out of this context — used to support denial, this is not my intention.

I am also not suggesting that we should not have boundaries with our own behavior (and I do believe that there is such a thing as a healthy, motivating relationship with limits). However, it is a very different thing to have a boundary because you want to love and honor something for the sacred opportunity and beauty it represents than it is to have a boundary because you are afraid; afraid that if you mess up, it will disappear, or afraid of the thing itself. When we fear our own actions, that clouds our ability to make good decisions. When we are acting from love, possibilities open that simply didn't exist previously.

What I **am** suggesting is a shift of consciousness with regard to the planet. This process may include a variety of steps, and for some of us that will include a level of honesty that allows us to admit that part of the buy-in to fear-based scenarios is layered on top of dynamics around abuse that we are deriving benefit from. We can't create something different until we admit there's something to change; just like being caught in a storm, the only way out is to go through it.

Evolution is a process, and it involves stages. There isn't

actually anything wrong with where we have been. This isn't a book about trashing where we have been or where we are now; it is a book about taking the next evolutionary steps. Many people have gained tremendous benefit from having looked through the doomsday filter, and much as I believe it is time to move on, the level of research that has gone into understanding the physical dynamics of pollution and the solutions of the physical plane are incredibly valuable.

I have personal ties with the doomsday filter. My father is an ecologist, one with both an amazing scientific mind and a deep intuition. I grew up in a household with a tremendously bright, committed and inspiring eco-role model. My dad does remarkable work, and he (along with the able help of my mom for a number of years) made a major contribution to the Great Lakes region being a safer, cleaner environment for hundreds of thousands of people. He also does land reclamation work on mine sites and landfills, and I am particularly proud to see him currently doing the ecological work on the Fresh Kills Landfill in New York, where the Twin Towers were taken. Dad is a doomsayer, and a damned fine one: articulate, focused, hard working, creative and gutsy.

The benefits of his work, and the work of thousands of other scientists, activists, moms and dads, and even corporations with a sense of real responsibility, need to be honored and acknowledged. Like every growth stage that we go through in a dynamic, evolutionary process, they were just the right things for that time. When Rachel Carson wrote *Silent Spring*, she did it in a completely different social and spiritual context than the one in which I am

7

writing. Her work is part of what laid the foundation for me to get to the point of being able to write *this* book. In another fifty years—give or take some—this book (and many others) will be old school and we will be on to the next evolutionary phase of thinking.

Things change. Needs change. Movements change.

Changes of all sorts begin and end in consciousness. We get the idea to do something, be something, change something, and only then can we do it, be it, change it. Change starts in new awareness, new awakenings of perspectives. Sometimes, consciousness takes a big leap—we know the names of some of those people who embodied those leaps—Einstein, Galileo, Jung, Gandhi, and in the environmental field, John Muir, Rachel Carson, and others. Our world is literally different because these people could articulate a new consciousness for us.

Consciousness is where it starts. In this moment, our collective consciousness has brought us to the point where the next gutsy, creative, articulate move looks to me like one away from doom saying and toward real faith in humanity. It is a move toward a perspective that says limitation thinking has served its purpose and worn out its usefulness. And this too is a phase we will pass through, on to something else I probably can't even imagine.

I welcome the day when so many people in so many different fields have repeated the ideas here that they are ho-hum and passé. The irony is that the evolution I am pointing us toward embraces some very, very old ideas, going back to Buddha and probably beyond. It is time for the great social movements of our time, including the environmental movement, to make a similar leap to the one personal growth advocates are already making—the leap away from limitations thinking and toward creative possibility. It is my intention to contribute to that leap.

The Birth of this Book

This book has its roots in four identifiable things: the early influence of my father's work; my personal growth work, particularly with a set of tools called Avatar[2] and my generally pagan sensibilities that tell me, in my bones, that the earth is sacred ground; a health scare with cervical cancer; and my pregnancy with my birth daughter Ananda who was adopted by close friends. I mentioned my dad above. Allow me to introduce you to the other three parts.

Avatar is that rarest of spiritual paths; while some paths encourage compassion and acceptance, and others encourage being fully responsible for your life and pro-active about creating what you want, the creator of Avatar understood (after a lot of personal trial and error) that a balanced and engaged life requires both. Paths that leave out one side of this equation have built-in pitfalls: acceptance, taken to an extreme, can lead to living with abuse or being passively unquestioning and calling it spiritual; being pro-active, taken to an extreme, can lead to running roughshod over others. By including

---

[2] Avatar is a superb set of personal tools; find out more at www.avatarepc.com

both, Avatar embodies the best of integrity, exploration and real growth. Rarely have I seen a spiritual technology that integrates the softening (and sense of humor) of acceptance with the creative aspects of spirituality as well as Avatar does, and I feel blessed to have found it at a young age.

Avatar has allowed me to explore some very interesting territory over the years with curiosity and groundedness, and one of my constant edges is with limits. Which limits that I experience in my life are self-imposed or cultural constructs? Which ones are inherent in having a body and being on a planet? What is the value of limits and in what ways are they a hindrance? When is it my integrity speaking and when am I just operating from fear? This stuff is particularly juicy for a sustainability advocate.

I have often found that when I get deeply honest with myself and am willing to take a few risks, things I've been experiencing as very solid limits melt away and I'm able to see possibilities where I previously saw none. Sometimes, this takes the form of discovering that I had such a moralistic judgment about something that, even though no one is being damaged by my pursuit of that possibility, I held myself back. Sometimes it is simply an unquestioned assumption about how the world works or how people are. I've wondered and explored and probed myself in the area of limited resources and limited capacity for humans to do good, and the results of that exploration have been an interesting mix of releasing things that I thought were solid fact and accepting some of the science of the planet as helpful. I'm still not 100% convinced that limits are "true" in

10

an absolute sense, but I do see that a belief in limits can be a good motivator to explore and ask ourselves what's really important to us. So Avatar deserves credit for being one strong root of this work.

Related to my exploration of limits is my own struggle with my physical health. In the past five years I've gone through two rounds of medical tests that indicated I was in the early stages of developing cervical cancer. Both times were deeply frightening to me (never mind that my doctor tells me women rarely die of this particular cancer these days; I was a hypochondriac growing up and the fastest way to scare the living hell out of me is to use the "C-word"). Both times, I've opted out of the standard medical advice involving cutting or burning out cells and turned instead to a combination of consciousness work and herbal healing and cleansing. Both times, my tests have been clear again after a relatively short period of concerted effort on my part and a willingness to face my fears without the crutch of invasive outside intervention.

Both rounds of this health scare have raised more questions for me about the relationship between physical being and consciousness. I have a complete faith in consciousness work (when we decide to apply it) in the realms of relationships, personal happiness and our ability to draw into our lives positive experiences (often to replace ones that were less than satisfying.) I've just seen it work too many times for my daughter-of-a-scientists' brain to deny the evidence in front of me. Where I've struggled more is in the seemingly "harder" realms of physical reality, including money and other physical manifestations, and the physical reality represented in

11

our relationship with the planet. And yet... two times of heading off cancer made me wonder: Is even the relationship we have with the planet and our conviction about the nature of nature malleable with consciousness work? The writing of this book has been one venue of exploring just this question, and the implications this question has for myself and other activists and sustainability teachers.

Finally, the fourth main influence in the writing of this book was a little surprise that manifested about a year and a half into the writing process, a baby girl by the name of Ananda Maya. After several years of being told by medical personnel that I couldn't get pregnant again (and being very much at peace with that news, and thoroughly content with my wonderful son as an only child) I suddenly found myself staring at a positive pee test in the fall of 2004. As it happened that two of my closest friends had been doing consciousness work *the same day* I got pregnant, clearing the way for them to adopt a baby, I suspected immediately that there were forces larger than me at work in manifesting this child. Ananda's creation, birth and subsequent adoption, and our ongoing relationship as family-outside-of-the-box have brought concepts like "miracle," "service to others," and "trusting your intuition even when the message that you are nuts is sorely tempting" out of the conceptual realm and into daily reality.

With Ananda in the world, and my relationship with her parents so very vibrant, my old stories about what humans are capable of have been turned on their heads. And that has had positive ripples into every arena of my life, including my sustainability work. I found that I could embrace risk-taking, hope and creativity in the face of what could have been a major life setback, and have discovered that there is a deep and abiding joy in getting bigger than my fear and contradictions: the biggest benefit to my work from my experience as Ananda's birth mother was a cat-worthy curiosity about what else I could apply this optimism to. You'll get more of her story later on in the book.

Reinventing the Old

As my own consciousness has lightened up and I've become more empowered and more self-aware, I have found that I've become increasingly less comfortable with the shrillness of the environmental movement. The blaming and scape goating, aimed at the bad guy d'jour (government agencies, corporations, people who drive SUV's, meat-eaters, Americans, etc.) became less and less appealing, especially as I started to get to know the real people in these categories and see them as friends. As my discomfort peaked, I made a humbling and unpleasant discovery: the shrillness and judgment I was seeing outside of myself was also inside me.

I knew I wasn't effective, but I got stuck at that point. I knew what I had been doing wasn't working, but the idea of applying consciousness work to the environmental field seemed fantastic. Relationships, I reasoned, are malleable, softer somehow than the world of science and fact that environmental work is often built upon.

I had a strong enough track record by this point around changing relationships through consciousness work that I had come to see it literally as the most practical approach I could take in those arenas, because it gave me the power to change even things that seemed to be, at least in part, outside of myself.

But this big, big planet, and the big, big crisis we have been creating on it seemed bigger than me, and bigger than consciousness work could really contribute to. I understood clearly how beliefs affect behavior, but I didn't yet get how they could affect the physical. The Earth seemed solid and concrete compared with the domain of human relations. *I hesitated to address environmental issues in a similar manner because I believed physical reality to be unaffected by consciousness.*

I suppose that is understandable, even if it did represent a decided lack of imagination. A planet after all, IS a big, complex thing compared to one small body! But my scares with cancer and my ability to stop creating something that seemed inexorable were slowly chipping away at that certainty. Somewhere in my consciousness, I was starting to have glimmers of taking that leap of imagination and faith and applying what I knew to the larger domain of eco-activism.

The Microcosm and the Macrocosm

In January 2004, I reviewed an Avatar course that specifically addresses collective consciousness and came home with a new level of respect for how an individual can affect the collective[3]. A couple of weeks later, I woke up one morning, to find myself sitting in an old creation of mine. I was tired and didn't feel well, on a day when I had real, important commitments to fulfill. I realized that I often used my body as an excuse to not do things, as a limiting factor in my own capacity. Being tired was an excuse to not really fully show up in my own life and do those things that I deemed important. So, I made a decision to do what I had been learning to do during the previous year and use my tools to shift my experience of being tired and run down. And it worked!

As I was doing my work, feeling and discreating[4], I had an epiphany (I know, everyone always says that at the beginning of books, but it really did feel like an epiphany). I realized — could feel, actually, viscerally — that there was a parallel between what I was experiencing in my personal life and the environmental movement.

The same beliefs that had me locked into seeing a body primarily as a limitation also apply to how we see the planet. In the same way that my limiting beliefs about having a body stopped me from creating what I wanted in my life — focusing attention on the limiting nature of my body rather than the opportunity it represents, and therefore creating evidence of that same limitation — our beliefs

---

[3] The Avatar Wizard Course.

[4] Discreating is an Avatar term for those processes that allow you to experience your creation without resistance so you can move them out of your consciousness. In this way, they no longer create unwanted experiences in your life.

about the planet can prevent us from seeing our time on the planet as a precious opportunity. Instead of being honored as a sacred opportunity, we treat both our bodies and the earth as a limit, *one that we simultaneously resent for its limited "nature" and feel a desperate need to save.* The same panicky feeling I felt when I really thought about my environmental work was present in my own body. The work I was doing with my body was suddenly a microcosm of the work we could be doing with the planet. The nice metaphor that I had explored years before, that my body is a reflection of the earth's body, suddenly took on new literal meaning for me.

What if, I asked myself, limitation is not the earth's inherent "nature" nor is it ours? What if it is a construct we have placed on it, one that shuts down our creativity at every turn? What if it only *looks* obviously true because we are so heavily invested in it? And how different would it look if we put the emphasis on thinking of being incarnate as an opportunity?

That moment of realization catalyzed my writing this book.

I handled my own "body as limit" creation and was able to get up and have a thoroughly productive and enjoyable day. I realized that we might be able to do similar things as a collective consciousness. The process is one of taking full responsibility for the roles we play in creating our lives as they are (and by this I mean both spiritually and tangibly) letting go of judgments about it and then *moving on.*

What would it mean to take full responsibility for the creation of the environmental crisis? Both the physical damage and the

16

practices that contribute to them, plus our attitudes that make it such a seductive thing to continue? We could, if we chose, handle the very real sickness the earth is experiencing as something we are responsible for but not trapped by, continue with the good work that is already in play to undo the damage we've already done, and move into a collective honoring of this planetary body we share, experiencing it as sacred ground for creative opportunity, and committing to stopping the habits that cause the damage in the first place.

There is certainly cleansing of the planet to be done, and much of that work will look roughly the same as what we are already doing. However, if the consciousness around *how we think* about the planet and interact with it doesn't change, neither will the damaging patterns. Like alcoholics, it isn't enough to lock up the bottles; we need to address the thought patterns and unhealthy emotional needs that prompt the behavior in the first place.

The process I am advocating begins with a collective shift in perception—that this shared body we call earth is a gift. No matter how well intentioned it may be, viewing the earth as a limitation is a form of desecration. Labeling the earth as limited diminishes the importance and value of something sacred and life giving. Desecrating something means to treat it in a way that makes it less worthy of our care—*the exact opposite of what activists intend.* As such, it is deeply disempowering to the goal it is meant to serve. This book offers a path for this shift in perception. There *are* other steps to be done, but this shift is one of them, and I believe that this is a missing

17

piece.

One of the parallel tracks of my exploration has offered a key realization: the healthier a person is (and I am now referring to emotional, empowered, or psychological health) the less likely they are to invest time and energy into limitations. As we become healthier and grow, we are naturally drawn to those things that are more expansive, those things that have more space for us to explore and grow further. Why would a growing being choose to invest herself into things that hold her small? And yet, what the environmental movement has offered (even demanded) is that people invest themselves in limitations thinking in order to be part of it. It's not surprising to me that we lose good people. Change the game, base it on a perspective of positive opportunity, and sane and healthy people will be willing and delighted to invest (or reinvest, as the case may be) time and energy into it.

On one level, this change is simply a process of aligning our attention with the practical stuff of empowering what serves us, instead of what holds us back. It is a leap that I believe we are ready to embrace. As a people, we have become more and more invested in being healthy in the latter part of the 20th century and on into this new century. It is our next evolutionary step as a people aware that we populate a planet.

To put my basic premise another way, *I believe that what we face in our relationship to the planet is not so much a crisis of limitation, as a crisis of personal responsibility and optimistic passion.* The current eco-movement focuses our attention on saving a limited thing, which for

me is ⸱ ⸱rsonal responsibility is the capacity
⸱ions are affecting those around us, to
⸱lame but rather to find creative solutions to
what ails us. Personal responsibility is a process we grow into, and
one that our mainstream culture in the United States discourages
more often than it encourages.

There is tremendous momentum and pressure in this country
to not be personally responsible. Responsibility has somehow gotten
associated with being weak or uncool. The typical law case, for
instance, asks people to put themselves into the best light and argue
"our case." This is not necessarily the full story, or most accurate
accounting of all that happened. Rather than taking full responsibility
for our own words and actions, we are encouraged to admit only
what makes us look good, and to create arguments that will win,
thereby having someone else assume responsibility for what we have
manifested in our lives. This isn't responsibility, and it is a cultural
level sickness in consciousness.

At the same time, many of us are looking outside ourselves—
to a partner or the government or somewhere else—for solutions to
our problems. The shift I am suggesting includes a shift toward seeing
us (and our colleagues in earth-nurturing work) as having the power,
creativity and capacity to contribute in a positive way through an
ethic of personal responsibility. While it might be nice if the
government were on board, waiting for that to happen is a waste of
precious time that we could be spending empowering ourselves and
others and learning the social skills required to live in a more

cooperative world. This evolution will be citizen-led.

The support for becoming more responsible may not come from mainstream sources. However, I have experienced that there are tremendous forces available to support our responsibility (even if they will only rarely be found on a television or political speech). The support for our real growth is generated internally and — if we are skilled at interpersonal relationships — within our communities. We create this support for ourselves by stepping into greater integrity and embracing those companions who are willing and able to join us in that pursuit.

As we become more responsible in our personal domain, it becomes increasingly uncomfortable to practice irresponsibility at other levels — including in our workplaces and as leaders. This is one of the keys to shifting our governments and corporations — to hold a space that says that the *people* who make up those governments and corporations are just as capable of responsible action as anyone else. I'm going to call it *personal* responsibility, even when we are talking about government agencies and large corporations. I do this because at the heart of governments and corporations, there are people. If there are ethical violations happening within these bodies, individual persons (real life people, just like you and me) are making those choices.

When we get to the point where we are unwilling to live unethical lives, we will not only manifest responsibility within the small domain of our own lives but we also manifest governmental and corporate responsibility. I believe that personal and corporate responsibility is the same thing, and breaking it into separate categories simply hands people an excuse to not take their ethics with them to work.

Personal responsibility is the domain in which we practice for being ethical leaders of others (be it politicians, business leaders, nonprofit managers, teachers, parents, etc.) And although it seems less impactful, this is where we start the journey toward corporate, governmental and indeed cultural transformation. The challenge is really holding space for someone to become more responsible, and it is a challenge because it requires letting go of the self-righteousness that we are often trained to embrace as activists. This is the challenge of the moment: to cultivate a real faith in humanity.

Ultimately, this is a book about optimism. This is not the sugarcoated, quick-to-act-without-care deflection of responsibility that sometimes gets called optimism. Rather, it is a deep, centered knowingness that the planet is headed down an evolutionarily bright path that we can speed up or slow down by our own actions. It's about the in-the-moment choice to embody hope. It's about *enjoying* responsibility, and greasing the wheels of our collective evolution by giving each other—not the "benefit of the *doubt*"—but the benefit of our faith and generosity. In real optimism, we see each other's actions as potentially beneficial; we don't assume the worst of each other.

Finally, this book is about passion. The deeply motivated sense of honoring something, being excited about it, being willing to commit our lives into its Service. What I see the world needing more than anything else is our aligned, optimistic, joyful passion.

What Else Is Here

This book is in part an "indictment" of the current situation. Because I take the view that we are in an evolutionary process, however, I'd like to offer the perspective that what we are actually doing is simply identifying the step that we are currently on, and how it no longer serves us. I frequently use the test of *usefulness* in my own evaluation of things. For our collective goal of living on a vibrant, healthy planet, is our current approach useful? That is, does it support this goal or undermine it?

You will also find here an exploration of a new vision for approaching environmental issues, which I refer to as *"enlightened eco-activism."* It is one of the many paths I believe we must walk, collectively and personally, in order to create a livable, viable culture in harmony with the planet. So the bulk of this book focuses on where I'd like to see us head.

Because it will help to understand my take on the current state of the environment if you have a brief glimpse into my philosophy on life in general, I'm going to share with you a few foundational beliefs that I hold, which are woven throughout book. All of these ideas are explored in more detail later on.

• The most important belief that I hold is that **we are responsible for our experiences.** We create our reality by the choices we make, the integrity of our actions and words, the beliefs we hold and the placement of our attention. This is true for the daily details of our lives, as well as for big picture things, such as our experience of our culture, our vision of the planet and even the decision to have been born in the first place. We are, ultimately, in the driver's seat. At this level of responsibility, there is an implied obligation to care for the planet as much as there is for your relationships with others, the health of your body, etc.

Whether this take on the world is "true" or not in some absolute sense, I can't tell you. But I believe that seeing ourselves as ultimately, deeply and joyfully responsible is by far the most practical and empowering perspective we can adopt: if you believe that you matter in the creation of your life, you are in a far better position to do something about it. If you believe that your choices, attention and beliefs don't matter, then you will spend your life feeling as if you are at the effect of circumstances around you (including the sometimes despair-inducing state of our planet) and this is not a very empowering place to live.

It's damn near impossible to make a difference when you believe that you can't. Not wanting to invest precious life energy in the impossible, I choose to believe that we can make a difference.

I also believe that this is true on a collective level. Cultures (which are really just groups of individuals) have power, and mass consciousness (which again, is just a conglomeration of us) has power. We do not alone create the state of the planet, but we contribute. We are not a sole product of our culture, but we have been influenced by it, and in turn have the power to influence it. The corollary, and a foundational belief for my work in sustainability, is that you cannot

23

separate cultural change from personal change.

• **Our level of influence depends on what domain[5] we are operating in**. In the personal domain, I believe that our influence is absolute: how I feel, how I respond, what I choose to do with my time... all of these things are in the personal domain, and the only one in charge of those things is me. When operating within the domain of others (the domain of one-on-one and small group relationships) we still have responsibility for our own responses, but we also have influence in the form of agreements. Often that means having to take on a perspective that is bigger and includes the needs and interests of others. Our influence in this domain is not so absolute. However, our creative power can be magnified here when we are dealing with people with whom we have a strong and sincere alignment. At the level of cultural or global domains, we have influence primarily in our ability and willingness to contribute. In these more collective domains, you increase your influence by creating partnerships and making connections with others.

No matter which domain we are talking about, there are two common themes. First, the level of influence we have is directly proportional to the amount of responsibility we are willing to take on in that domain. Second, the creation of our lives is like a blend of science and art. There are some actions you can take that will produce predictable results (and in this way, it is a sort of "science"). And then

---

[5] For a thorough and thoughtful discussion of domains, see *The Avatar Master's Handbook*, by Harry Palmer, 1997.

there are things that you create through experimenting, building skills up, and being willing to let go and allow the creation to unfold with its own beauty and adventure. This is the "art" of life. There's a learning curve involved in figuring out how to combine this science and art. Your own learning is best served by hopping in and doing it with intent, clarity, passion, a willingness to make mistakes and the strength to keep going.

• **I choose to spend most of my time in a state of optimism.** I find that when I combine optimism with its sister state of passion, I have a formula that allows me to be most effective[6]. I have a relatively low tolerance for pessimism, blame and inaction, primarily for reasons that I consider to be practical.

• **It is only by accepting the world exactly as it is in this moment that we are able to move ahead.** This is also true of ourselves. To be ruthlessly honest about the state of things and at the same time compassionately forgiving of our faults (which are truly universal) opens the doorway to evolving. This book is my attempt at honesty about a movement for which I care deeply, and about evolution, both personal and as a movement.

---

[6] My definitions of optimism and passion are probably not the most common ones, and I'll explore this in depth later. For now, suffice it to say that when we take responsibility for our lives, optimism and passion are our natural state—and it is highly creative and resilient. The better our ability to choose our own emotional state at any given time (one of the gifts of Avatar and other sincere, deeply held spiritual paths) the more able we are to maintain and use it.

• **Finally, I am unabashedly spiritual about environmental issues**. I believe that we have reached a point where spirituality is actually the most practical approach we can take. It is time to introduce compassion, understanding and an honoring of the sacredness of life into political dialogue. Without these components, we set ourselves up to repeat the same old patterns, which will keep us headed in the same direction we are going right now. One definition of insanity (and I wish I knew who to credit this to, but I don't) is "doing the same thing and expecting different results". Anything that helps us to sincerely grow out of old patterns that no longer serve us is a practical thing, and compassion and connection are two examples of what needs to be incorporated into our political work at this time.

Chapter 1: Playground Earth

Do you have a body? (Sometimes I get pretty in my head and I need to check. So far, though, I've always come up with "yes" to this one...) It seems to me that we all made a fundamental choice—to be here, now, in a body. For the sake of this discussion, I'm going to refer to this decision to have a body, in this place and time, as our *fundamental choice*.

Here, on this planet, we have certain opportunities and challenges both.

Now, at this historical moment, as in every historical moment, there are particular questions in front of us collectively.

In bodies, we are affected by things that we wouldn't be otherwise, and we get to experience things that we couldn't otherwise.

So, to be here, now, in a body implies certain things—as with every choice we make to experience something, there are consequences to these particular choices. I believe that we all made this choice, and we did it for our own reasons. As I stated in the introduction, I have a certain spiritual perspective that says we are fully responsible for our lives. I believe that we set this life up with certain basic — very basic, in this case — parameters in which we chose to live this life. The baseline question for each of us as evolving beings is this: how do we become fully responsible for our choices?

There are thousands of implications to that last question: hours of exploring to be done, will power to be developed, goals to be set and met, honesties to be had, joys to be experienced and fulfilled. These are all parts of the great exploration of life. Having said that, and encouraged you on your merry way to discovering those things for yourself, I'm going to focus (here, now, in this book) on one of the answers: *to be fully responsible for the choice to be here, now, in a body implies a responsibility to take care of the planet.*

If you didn't want to deal with what has gotten labeled the "global ecological crisis," I believe you would have picked a different here, a different now, or something that didn't involve a body.

How to deal with global ecological issues is one of the themes of our time[7]. From a purely selfish perspective, deciding to have a body and then abusing its home is a direct path to suffering. And while it does seem that some of us came here to experience suffering,

---

[7] There are other themes as well, such as globalization, alternative economics, human rights, etc. I'm focusing on ecological issues because it is the theme I am most articulate about, and therefore the most able to contribute to our collective growth. But by all means, explore what else might be basic reasons for you being here, now, in a body!

it is not the wisest of approaches to life, nor do I believe it is necessary to prolong the experience.

Within the fundamental choice of here/now/with body, each of us also made other, smaller choices. These include being born into a certain culture, gender, social class, etc. Each of these has its own implications. In the context we are talking about here (of looking at our relationship to the planet) it simply means that we have opted for different roles and different paths toward responsibility.

For someone born into a wealthy business-oriented American family, the path to real responsibility for our fundamental choice may look one way and include certain lessons and identities and decisions. For a poor child who is growing up in India on a rural farm, these responsibilities are going to involve whole other lessons and wisdoms and growth and perspectives. And for the poor American and wealthy Indian, the themes will be different again...

We are all integrating consciousness—we are all in this together.

What part did you come here to play? How is your growth path on the way to real responsibility linked to your fundamental choice?

This is where our paths suggest the particulars of our growth. No person is going to exactly the same place as any other person, and no one will answer the call of their life in quite the same way as anyone else. I believe, however, that it is imperative that we do each answer the call.

29

101 Cool Things about Having a Body

chocolate ice cream; walking along a river; the joyfully controlled chaos of a circus; the smell of lilac bushes in spring bloom; holding hands; pesto, on anything; watching a toddler bump around the room; campfires; hot sun on a beach; the smell of a pine forest; city bustle on a Friday night; country silences; a really good book that keeps you up at night; long, slow playful foreplay; the sound of hundreds of frogs on a spring night; jumping jacks 'til you drop; crunchy cucumbers and juicy berries; dappled sunlight in the woods; foot massages; watching the changing spectrum of colors while a bruise heals (after it stops hurting!); being able to pick things up; cozy socks on a cold day; hot tea, iced tea; fresh mangoes; using the body to give pleasure to someone else's body; crunchy tortilla chips; strolling an open air market; having a mind to store memories and being able to pull them out again; babies squirming in the belly; fingers and eyes to surf the internet; live music that moves you to tears; live music that moves you to dance; bird watching; planting a garden, watching it grow and eating fresh peppers; reading Calvin and Hobbes to a kid, and watching him laugh so hard he can hardly breathe; the feeling of hands on a drum head; legos; riding an elephant through the jungle in the rain; really good organic latte; northern lights; feeling the wind when you run; seeing the wind ripple poplar leaves; the happy exhaustion of a good day's work; sleeping, dreaming and waking up; birthday cake, birthday parties and birthday presents; the first spring thaw; giving birth and looking into the eyes of a newborn; watching the glowing tiny jelly fish at the aquarium;

the feeling of wet clay slipping past your hands as it spins on a pottery wheel; feeling happy for no apparent reason; a really good cry; flying kites; being able to hold crayons; the soft glow of candlelight filtering into eyes; waking up to the sound of cranes calling; funny little vegetables like tomatillos; waking up next to a beloved partner and knowing you have the whole day together; the change of the air right before it rains; singing along with your favorite songs in the car; clearing up a misunderstanding with a friend; playing in a sandbox; purring kittens, hyper playing kittens; growing older and liking it; hiking to the top of mountain and getting in a natural hot spring; the feel of a well feng-shuied home; fresh flowers; reflections on the smooth surface of a lake on a windless day; the sound of loons talking to each other; that shade of blue right before the sky turns to night; silk against the skin; good wine; cooking a meal for people you love, and lingering over it together; the feeling in your body after a good fast; sun dried tomatoes and green chili; a stimulating conversation with a new friend; camping out; a fancy night on the town; cuddling with your dog; the spacious feel of a day off after a big project is complete; nonsense fridge magnet poetry that is oddly resonant; getting a sincere and unexpected apology; horse back riding; that first moment you realize you are falling in love; the absolute silence of being underwater; feeling awestruck; cheese cake; discovering something new about someone you've known for years; finally reaching your toes after weeks of stretching; the last moment of consciousness before you slip into sleep; cat-napping in the sun

Life is change. Life is mistakes, and unexpected turns, and what we do with them. Activism is — ideally — personal, grounded, here, practical. From one perspective, being an enlightened activist is simply having a willingness to accept that part of human nature is that we are beings who mess up, and that we need to be willing to repair whatever damage we have done, individually and collectively. It seems that as long as we are incarnating, we'll need our activist selves to pay attention to the impact of our actions, and offer corrections as necessary. Sometimes it seems like we think that activism is something that we do until we mold a perfect world, at which point we'll make ourselves obsolete. It seems to me, however, that as long as we have bodies, we'll need activism to keep us collectively ethical.

Activism, in my world, is simply having a conscience and a commitment to act on its behalf.[8] This is a gentler take on activism than many have, more like a caring guardian than a righteous warrior.

Playground Earth

Bring to mind that thing which you most deeply desire for your life. Feel what it would feel like to have that. Now picture it in

---

[8] Later in this book, we'll look more closely at the developed version of these two things, where conscience becomes vision and the inspired commitment to act becomes passion.

your mind, and ask yourself this question: *Where am I?*

I have no idea what it is that you just thought of and for the sake of this little exercise it doesn't much matter. I believe I can safely tell you one thing about it (unless it involves perpetual astral travel, or being dead) and that is that you need a *place* to do your dream. That place is the earth. Regardless of our goals, our desires, our passions, our commitments, the one thing they all have in common is requiring a physical space.

I call it the playground. If you are going to play, you need a playground. Playground Earth.

So it behooves us to take care of the planet, regardless of the specific content of our goals, because the Earth is our playground. Poison the playground, use up the sand, and it doesn't matter why you think you are here, or if you think you care about the planet. That's it. Game over.

This is a creative partnership. The Earth provides a place to play, resources, inspiration, beautiful sites to keep us company, healthy boundaries, and a host of other things. We provide the games, the goals, the interesting happenings. A life well lived requires both the playground and the play.

If we are able to see the planet and ourselves in light of this creative partnership, then we can shift our eco-activism to be celebratory, fun and inspiring collaborations between people who know how to get things done[9]. Shock value wears off, and sucks our

---

[9] If you do not consider yourself to be someone who knows how to get things done, that's where to start: set goals you can achieve, do them and build some confidence.

energy by fixing our attention on stuck images and emotions. That image you just can't get out of your head (which may have been put their by a fellow activist on a billboard or a commercial) is occupying space that could be better used for creative thinking.

On the other hand, the memory of real closeness, creativity and inspiration spurs us on to greater heights. The latter gives us energy to keep going, a visceral reminder that life can be good. Creativity is just more fun than guilt, and you are more likely to pursue a repeat experience that involved fun than you are to pursue more opportunities to feel guilt. Besides, real community and partnership are easier to maintain than alliances based on common enemies because *maintaining the illusion of enemies requires energy of its own to sustain.*

From this perspective, actions such as the annual puppet parade in Minneapolis, the visible, community-oriented activism of City Repair in Portland, Oregon, and the beautiful, nurturing and artistic buildings at Earthaven Ecovillage in North Carolina are all examples of good eco-activism. Direct, simple, confidence-building teachings are preferable to endless facts and heavy predictions. Art, fun and food are good mediums; really anything that inspires is a good medium. Dogmatic lectures, angry confrontation and drama hold very small places in a more nurturing movement that builds community and enrolls powerful people.

Then join an alliance of others who have taken the time to create themselves as competent doers.

The most important resource we have is each other. This is important, so I am going to run the risk of insult and repeat myself: *The most important resource we have is each other.*

In the mainstream of the United States, we are driven by materialism and individualism. To some extent, this is simply a natural developmental stage. Humans need to develop a certain level of healthy ego, a capacity to independently take care of ourselves, and enough attention on the material plane that we are nurtured and aren't draining others around us to get our basic needs met. This is a good, healthy thing.

Where it has crossed over a line—and one that is subtle enough to be hardly detectable in our daily lives—is in a belief that material pursuits are the end game.

We have a lot of attention in our culture on material wealth, comfort and security. When viewed from the perspective of evolutionary consciousness, it could be said that we are collectively completing that experience, and preparing to evolve into the next thing. When a person is ready to move on from something, there can be a need to max out the experience, exhausting it and making it uninteresting to hang on to. How many of us party hard in our late teens and early twenties, only to wake up (slowly or suddenly) and decide that it isn't much fun anymore and it is time to get a new hobby? This is a natural growth process: we exhaust our interest in one thing and move on to the next, all without anyone having to preach it to us. Healthy, growing people do this all the time.

Cultures do the same thing. It hardly seems possible that it is coincidence that the US has generated some very powerful spiritual leaders and new personal growth technologies in the past twenty years, or that the Intentional Communities[10] Movement is as strong as it is here. The people at the heart of these movements in the US are here as a natural consequence of our having maxed out selfishness, materialism and individualism. Culturally, many of us are starting to get bored with the old game and are looking for something new: spiritual development, personal growth, real community and service to others. It is my belief that this is exactly *because* we have such a mainstream focus on materialism and individualism, and not, as many people say, in spite of these things.

There is a necessity and a real gift to having gone through the phase we are now completing. As people who have done the competent moneymaking and focused success track move on to these new endeavors, they are energizing social and spiritual movements. These people bring a standard of achieving more into our movements. People (and cultures) who try to skip the step entirely of being able to competently, independently care for ourselves in the material plane are going to struggle when it comes time to follow a path of deliberately creating community, spiritual capacities and service to

---

[10] Intentional communities are simply groups of people with a shared goal who live and/or work together. I'll talk more about IC's later, but for now the point is that they can be powerful venues for social and cultural exploration. Some groups form in reaction to a dominant culture they feel is stifling or misguided, others to fully explore some aspect of life together, and still others just to know their neighbors better. All of them that I'm familiar with, however, are pushing the envelope in some way on human relations, and that is all to the good.

others.[11]

In intentional communities, we see this all the time—people who are not able to independently care for their physical plane needs get together and try to create something collectively, only to fail painfully because of those very things they have resisted developing in themselves—there isn't enough competence around money or dealing with bureaucracy to be able to manifest something collectively. This isn't the only reason why they fail, but it is a common one.

Both sides of this seeming dichotomy (the material and the spiritual) are essential if we want to sustain and grow a movement of any sort. In the environmental movement (and other nonprofit communities) we generally have so many judgments on our more professional companions and on money that we sabotage our own growth, and are barely scraping by financially and energetically.

An example from my own path. A few years ago, I did a round of personal work on the topic of money. I had gotten tired of doing good work and having huge stress about feeding my son and myself. I just got sick of it. Sick enough that I was willing to uncover any crap in my own consciousness that was blocking my flow of

---

[11] In some other parts of the world, where folks are still struggling for clean water and enough food, material pursuit is necessary. From that perspective, the luxuries of your average American look pretty good. Having pursued the material, though, many of us have discovered that it doesn't make us happy, or secure, or alive.

money. I was in debt, grumpy and stressed; in short, I had maxed out the experience of righteous poverty, and was ready to move on.

After a bit of digging around I hit on a pattern I'd been running. I had always prided myself on never having had a "real job". I had pieced together a living by working for low wages at co-ops and nonprofits, or free-lanced teaching and doing tarot and astrology readings for a living, but I'd never had a straight job that would have "compromised my values". I (arrogantly) considered myself to be morally squeaky clean in the money department. That was one piece.

What was more interesting to me was what was underneath that: I started to see all the ways that I was using the "squeaky-clean-social-change-wonder-woman" identity as a social bargaining chip. So long as I was poor and morally above reproach, I could walk into just about any activist group and use that as alternative culture social power – I had never compromised. And more often than not people within those organizations would indeed look up to me for having done my life that way.

Unfortunately, the result of carrying this around in my consciousness was twofold. First, I was being an arrogant prig, turning off people who had lived more "mainstream" (or just more financially abundant) lives. Not surprisingly, that was practically everyone I came into contact with. I was alienating potentially valuable allies. Second, I was keeping myself poor and struggling financially, which was not only self-abusive, but abusive to my son as well. (It's amazing what we will do to ourselves and others when we are getting an ego fix out of it.)

In the year after I handled this stuff in my own consciousness, I paid off all my debts, made enough money to take the summer off and play, and relaxed considerably, all doing work I loved for nonprofits. One of the lessons I took away from this is that it isn't necessarily true that being poor and doing good works go hand-in-hand... unless we are holding something in our consciousness that sets it up that way. And it isn't of service to any of us.

In the environmental movement in particular there is an interesting parallel that takes place. We don't create abundance for ourselves personally (which is a lack of full responsibility for ourselves and requires others to take care of us) and then we preach the doctrine that the earth isn't abundant (and needs us to take care of Her). The consciousness of the activists is exactly mirrored in the dogma we are spouting about the earth.

The new question—the one really worth asking is: did the consciousness come first, and is this "save game" we are advocating for in our perspective about the "limited earth" actually as real as we make it?

To look at it from another angle, say I stress myself out in my work and don't make enough money to pay for my health maintenance. I am setting myself up to be a burden on someone else if I get seriously ill (which I may very well do given my work and stress load.) In 1990, I quit an eco-activist job only after I passed out from the cumulative exhaustion of six months of 70-hour weeks. How is that sustainable? I shudder to think what would have happened if I hadn't quit. I was advocating for something I didn't embody:

responsibility, sustainability and health.

The point is that our personal (and collective) consciousness is getting reflected in, and perhaps even projected onto, the Earth. If we judge abundance as bad or unimportant, then everything around us that has the potential to provide real abundance — read: the planet — will look tainted. More importantly, we feed energy into those things that aren't supporting abundance by making them more real.

Earth as Lover

Here's an interesting exercise: what if we thought of the Earth as we do a lover? Imagine you have a lover or partner, or if you have one right now, put some attention on that relationship. Now, ask yourself: would I like to be treated by my beloved the way that I treat the earth?

To enter into a sacred partnership with anyone or anything is a profound experience. Look honestly at how you relate with other humans that you are intimate with, and how you relate to the Earth. Are there some parallels?

The point here is to begin seeing your relationship with the planet as being as immediately impactful as the relationships we have with other intimates in our lives. What is more intimate than our relationship with the Earth? Who else feeds you every time you eat, provides constant companionship and beauty, won't ever abandon you, and has been with you every second of your life? Indeed, who else provided the very stuff of your flesh?

Interpersonal relationships can be a learning ground for attitudes and skills that nurturing the earth requires. By the same token, becoming more conscientious and loving toward the earth can have a profound impact on how you relate to other humans. This is because *consciousness is consciousness and relationships are relationships.* Regardless of whether we are talking interpersonal or global, most of us have patterns that carry over into all aspects of life. One doesn't cease to be fundamentally generous or fundamentally intellectual, for instance, just because the scale or type of relationship is different.

Perhaps you have done a lot of work on relationships; if so, what lessons and skills can you now apply to how you interact with the planet? Having a really vibrant, healthy relationship is a mix of fearless engagement, self-responsibility, appreciation, honesty, not using the other as an excuse for your behavior, and a willingness to feel good and be creative. These things are also the mark of a powerful and honest sustainability advocate. I invite you to play with this metaphor and find ways to begin seeing the earth as another important being you relate to, call on for support and lavish affection on. It's sure a lot more fun than guilt and worry.

Chapter 2: Gaia, Revisited

We are all connected; some would say we are all one. Often metaphysics predates science in understanding some aspect of how life works. We often find that over a period of time that which was once considered metaphor is physical reality as well.

I can't explain the mechanics of how a scientist would explain the tangible link between the physical plane and consciousness. But there are some interesting crossovers happening right now.

I am moved by the work of Dr. Masaru Emoto in Japan. Dr. Emoto has taken water samples and "showed" the samples pictures or words, frozen them, then photographed the crystal structure of each sample. The structure of the water actually changes. Somehow, words and concepts DO affect the physical plane. He has also observed the structure change as different people are looking at the water samples. Dr. Emoto says, "... a gaze of good intentions will give courage, an evil gaze will actually take it away."[12]

If simply *looking* can change the physical plane, it seems to me that it behooves us to take into account our attitudes and words and how they may be reinforcing those things we would prefer to not have in our lives. Expectations, beliefs and attitudes matter — and not just to our own well-being. They spill over in a very tangible way to the world around us.

When you gaze upon the world, do you see it as fragile, limited, dying? Or is your gaze one of appreciating the beauty, abundance and life force of the world? What are you empowering? If Dr. Emoto is right, this matters.

James Lovelock articulated the Gaia concept — the idea that the earth and its inhabitants combine to form a complex organism, a being in and of itself — in the 1960's. It is one that has slowly gained credibility over the years as more and more scientists and lay people have begun taking this view. When we view the planet as an organism, we allow ourselves a perspective that says that damaging one part of the planet weakens the viability of the whole. (And also that our individual health contributes directly to the planet's health.) We have a way to wrap our minds around the idea that we are truly connected.

---

[12] Dr. Emoto's work was recently popularized by the film *What the Bleep Do We Know!?* which, whether you think it was a "good movie" or not, certainly provides considerable food for thought for the spiritually adventurous. The quote appears in an article by Dr. Emoto in the Winter 2004 edition *of Light of Consciousness* magazine.

But before Lovelock came Carl Jung. Jungian psychology offered the first real articulation of the idea that consciousness is an interconnected whole. We are able to access the "collective unconscious" because of this interconnectedness. The collective unconscious is like a vast web, or an ocean, the metaphor Harry Palmer uses in *Living Deliberately*[13]. Palmer says that every belief we have is like a drop in a vast ocean, and it affects the collective consciousness, minutely yet perceptibly. Add a drop, and you change things. You open up the possibility, perhaps, of pursuing something new, just by the shift within your own consciousness.

I submit that the Gaia concept and the idea of collective consciousness are simply two levels of the same thing: one has physical form and one doesn't, but they interrelate. Consciousness generates physical beingness, and physical beingness can be measured to determine the state of consciousness on the planet. It is actually quite convenient to have both—what manifests in physical form allows us to get an accurate read on what is going on in the unseen realm of consciousness. And, even better, we can head off certain unwanted happenings if we catch them early enough, while we are still just toying with them in consciousness.

Healers worldwide are recognizing more and more that consciousness matters in the healing process. Louise Hay[14] has made a whole career out of healing through changing consciousness. Her

---

[13] *Living Deliberately*, by Harry Palmer, 1994.

approach creates what is widely referred to as "miracles" on a regular basis. My own experience of heading off a serious illness by taking the combined approach of cleansing my body (to undo the damage already done on the physical plane) and addressing my consciousness (to stop generating the disease) was enough to convince me that there is a much more direct relationship between consciousness and physicality than most of us are aware.

Physical reality is the dense, slower-moving cousin of consciousness. It does take physical work and cleansing to undo physical damage once it is done, unless we are willing to live with the physical plane's own timeline. But simply addressing the physical alone will not change the underlying problems. This is where the sustainability movement would benefit from broadening its focus to include consciousness work.

If you want to know the overall direction of consciousness on the planet, pick up a copy of this year's version of the Worldwatch Institute's State of the World report. You'll find that, compared to the earliest State of the World books, some things have improved, while others have continued to go downhill. This is an exact reflection of the consciousness of the world. Someone who is being either optimistic or in denial might tuneinto all the amazing projects of hope in the world. Others with a more cynical view on the world can point to environmental disasters, wars, etc. and come to the conclusion that

---

[14] Hay's various books include *You Can Heal Your Life*, which connects specific thought patterns with specific diseases and is an excellent guide to getting started on a healing process.

we already have one foot in hell. The irony is that humanity seems to be simultaneously finding ways to perfect cruelty and arrogance, and exploring the heights of enlightenment in larger numbers every year. Perhaps the extremes are more available in more abundance than ever before; or perhaps, in the age of mass communication, they are simply easier to access.

So what it comes down to, really, is choice. What are you going to focus on?

If you knew — with absolute certainty — that your actions, your intentions, your very thoughts would result in a physical manifestation that mirrored them, could you find in this a natural, self-regulating approach to environmental ethics?

Toxic thoughts are reflected in toxic waste. Emotionally abusive relationships, based on subjugation and selfishness, are reflected in abuse to the planet. Burning your candle at both ends will eventually burn out the very ground we walk upon. There is no separation between individual consciousness and mass consciousness; they only seem separate because of the difference in scale. There is no separation between individual health and Gaia's health. This collective, called earth, is simply the sum total of every individual consciousness, in each moment.

I learned years ago in my feminist pagan circles to see my body as the goddess' body, and that the earth herself is goddess incarnate. At the time I thought that was a pretty, new-agey thought. I have since come to see that it is neither that, nor is it old-world superstitious nonsense. It is a literal statement that encompasses a

47

spiritual perspective that my sacredness and the earth's are the same. But it also holds that my treatment of my small world will contribute that exact energy to the treatment of the larger world. It is an invitation to see the blood and body of Christ all around us, and to care for that sacred being in our everyday actions.

How many modern diseases are somehow linked to excessive toxins in the physical environment? How many of us are channeling "environmental sensitivities" in the small spheres of our own bodies, expressing the earth's toxicity in our personal physical beings? And how many more of us carry a vaguely-symptomed burn out, reflective of the slow loss of vibrancy in our soil and waters — body and blood of the planet?

Labeling these things "metaphorical" opens the door to diminishing the importance of what they tell us. Another option is to see them as accurate reflections of each other, small and large-scale manifestation of the same things. Our bodies and the planet, running on parallel tracks.

Now look at consciousness. Modern America is overrun with depression, boredom and fear. These are the psychic and psychological equivalents of immune systems burning out, low level lack of health and vibrancy, and toxicity. We use drugs (legal and illegal) to numb us out that much more, but that isn't the answer. There have been reports of detectable levels of anti-depressants in some city water systems, presumably because so many people pee it out and flush it down[15]. For me, this is a creepily literal manifestation of how connected our personal psychological health is to the physical vibrancy of the planet. It's almost a cosmic joke, except that it isn't particularly funny: our (psychological) depression is quite literally polluting the (physical) blood of the planet.

So, is this relationship causal or just reflective? I'll leave that debate to others. Better yet, I invite people to actively explore it for themselves.

Either way, the action suggested is the same—address them as two sides of the same coin. Stop viewing ecological activism as something strictly tied to the physical plane, and begin to integrate consciousness work (our own personal consciousness work first) into what we are doing as activists. Change minds, change attitudes, and change your waste management practices all at once. This is holistic, long-term, *sustainable* activism.

---

[15] I don't know if this is literally true or not, and I haven't been able to confirm if it is really an "urban legend". But the fact that it is at all believable is in and of itself worth noting; we wouldn't be surprised if our depression—and the willingness to drug ourselves out of it—has reached that point. Isn't that creepy?

Chapter 3: "Not to be too spiritual about this, but..."

"There is a perverse form of contemporary violence in which the idealist fighting for peace by non-violent methods most easily succumbs: activism and overwork. The rush and pressure of modern life are a form, perhaps the most common form, of its innate violence. To allow oneself to be carried away by a multitude of conflicting concerns, to surrender to too many demands, to commit oneself to too many projects, to want to help everyone in everything, is to succumb to violence. The frenzy of the activist neutralizes work for peace. It destroys the fruitfulness of work, because it kills the root of inner wisdom which makes work fruitful."

— Thomas Merton, *Conjectures of a Guilty Bystander*

For a couple years, I taught with a group of amazing beings collectively referred to as the Sustain Ability Trust. I remember quite distinctly a man in one of our classes beginning a comment with, "Not to be too spiritual about this, but..."

For me, this is an example of one of the struggles many of us face. There is both an urge toward a compassionate, self-responsible

51

(read: spiritual) perspective, as well as an odd sense of shame around it. Sitting in a room of people with no real sense of where any of the others were coming from, this guy was brave enough to offer a potentially risky perspective. But he couldn't quite do it without half apologizing.

We can't apologize. We can't afford to cut ourselves off from the deep inherent ethics of self-honesty and self-responsibility, the "root of inner wisdom which makes work fruitful" as Thomas Merton so eloquently writes. Maintaining that perspective is a profoundly spiritual act. Years of an environmental movement based on blame and punishment have not essentially altered what we are actually doing to the planet. We need to take a next step.

There is always hesitancy when we are ahead of the mainstream curve and starting to explore a new paradigm. I am an advocate for compassion and self-responsibility: in a context where we are currently trained to blame others, people who follow this path are not only bucking the current trend, but we are also making ourselves vulnerable. When you say, "Well, what about me? What's my responsibility?" it's kind of like painting a target on your chest. (Worse, try, "What about us?") We open ourselves to criticism by being willing to admit that maybe the current state of things does have something to do with us. And if you are the only one in the room copping to it, it can be very easy to become the scapegoat. Admitting fault at any level around people accustomed to blaming can be a risky business! (A friend of mine describes this as the "feeding frenzy" and the image of piranha it invokes is not one we ought to be proud of.)

Self-responsibility in the area of sustainability does not mean that we cut ourselves off from dialogue. It doesn't mean that we let others get away with destructive acts. It *does* mean that we have first done our own work in those same areas. This allows us to do our addressing of others not as enemies or accusers, but as real, mistake-making, working-toward-our-own-solutions human companions on a journey.

I lived for years in Michigan, which doesn't require emissions testing to get your car registered. In spite of having a strong awareness of vehicle emissions and the problems associated with them, it simply never occurred to me to get my car tested. It wasn't until I moved to New Mexico, which requires testing, that I realized I had been being pretty hypocritical.

Here's the hypocritical part. During the same time that I lived in Michigan, I was very active in my criticism of the local incinerator, whose managers didn't get anything tested they didn't have to. My blood would boil every time I'd see the smoke chugging out of the pipes — usually while driving my not-particularly-fuel-efficient big old car somewhere (that's the extra irony) to teach an environmental program (irony #3).

An interesting thing happens when we are out of integrity with our own ideas of what is right. We get defensive of our own behavior, and hyper critical of similar behavior in others. We lose our ability to see clearly what is happening because our own consciousness is being pulled in two directions — one by a positive

53

urge to do well, and one by shame that we aren't actually following it. Divided within ourselves, it's easy to get confused and unsure of our footing. And when people are unsure of ourselves, we make more mistakes. Our discernment is thrown off, and it becomes very difficult to see clearly what needs to be corrected and how to correct it.

So here's the lesson: if I want to address the purple smoke from the pipes at the local incinerator, I will be far more effective if I first get my own tailpipe tested, and, if need be, corrected. This creates a solid foundation for me to speak from.

To a certain extent, this is simply a matter of efficient use of our activist energy. No one likes hypocrisy, and very few people will respond well to a hypocrite trying to correct their behavior. So it becomes of the utmost importance that we get our own stuff handled. If we don't, we doom ourselves and the issues we care about to failure (or at best, mediocrity) because eventually the house will fall down without a good foundation.

Strong, powerful, honest, ethical people are the foundation of a strong, powerful, honest, ethical movement.

Growing into Responsibility

This is the point where the argument, "But the impact of an incinerator is so much bigger than my car's impact" usually comes up, and from a certain perspective, that is true. The question I am addressing here, however, is a somewhat different one. We are talking about how much *responsibility* we are willing to sincerely handle, and learning to handle a larger and larger amount of responsibility is a *process.*[16] It's the old biblical adage about taking the plank out of one's own eye before attacking someone for having a splinter in theirs.

As a more obvious illustration, you wouldn't give your average 18-year-old responsibility for a multimillion-dollar company. It would not only be a setup for failure for the enterprise, but it would also be an act of cruelty. She'd need to learn how to handle greater responsibility as she went along. This has nothing to do with her inherent talents, brains or work ethic. In order to run that business well, she'd have to be able to balance all sorts of factors and jobs. When given a chance to *grow into* responsibility (as opposed to what is often referred to as "sink or swim" learning) becoming more responsible is a natural, comparatively effortless progression.

This isn't just relevant for businesses. Another path toward responsibility might be that I first learn to be responsible for myself, then myself and a cat, then myself and a cat and a child, and only then for a larger community[17]. The lessons I learn along the way

---

[16] This willingness to handle responsibility goes hand-in-hand with the distinction I am trying to draw between having a crisis of limitation versus a crisis of responsibility. When we are operating from limitation, we tend to spend a lot of energy figuring out what and who is wrong (blame); when we focus on responsibility, it is about how much integrity we can uphold.

[17] My wonderful editor, Elizabeth, tells me that I ought to cite a Sandra Bullock movie called *28 Days* for this one. The movie is about a woman in recovery, and part of the program she is in includes sending the participants home with a plant to care for. If the plant lives, they are allowed to get a pet, etc. I haven't seen the movie

would prove invaluable, and would be the building blocks of my success.

Do you have someone in your life whom you admire because they just seem to have it all together? I can almost guarantee that person spent some time figuring it out, learning to handle the level of responsibility that looks (and may even be) easy. Everyone starts somewhere. What may seem remarkable to you is simply the result of them being ahead of you in the process of growth and in their assumption of responsibility. Ability, discernment and willingness are all skills that are built up over a period of time. Then, once we have a role in a bigger picture, we are able to assume that responsibility and carry it easily without it being the struggle that it would have been five years (or even six months) before.

Now notice the behavior of someone who has more responsibility than they can actually handle. They might be defensive when questioned, criticized or overwhelmed. When we find ourselves in over our heads, most of us have a tendency to act in a less than admirable fashion. We might make stuff up when we don't really know the answer, or try to hide our mistakes. It is not an easy, competent feel; it is, in fact, wrought with insecurities and often tinged with a bit of desperation.

The same lessons that make for smart business practices and competent pet ownership can be applied to our activism. Addressing how we are out of integrity in our relationship with the earth in the

---

myself, but it sounds pretty right on (and hey, if you can't trust your editor, who can you trust?)

small sphere of our personal lives is the first step in being able to address a larger level without strain, and with a high degree of effectiveness. Remember that example I described where I had a job that literally burned me out? I fell prey to Thomas Merton's "modern violence" of the activist by working 70-hour weeks, eating a lot of take-out food, not being able to pay my bills, and essentially destroying a good relationship in the process by abusing the generosity and love of a very good man.

I wasn't yet responsible for my own life. At the same time, I was going door-to-door asking people to help me make corporations responsible for their toxic waste spills. On a metaphorical level, I hadn't yet cleaned up the toxic, damaging stuff in my own life. It wasn't until the day that I literally keeled over that I started to get a clue that something was out of whack!

My body knew what my mind was still unwilling to admit: I wasn't yet in a position to responsibly address anything outside of myself, because I hadn't yet learned to embody responsibility at the level I was asking others to embody it. It is unsurprising to me that we live in a culture that devalues the sacredness of our own bodies and that this is reflected in the environmental damage we are causing to the planet all around us. Again, the state of the planet reflects our beliefs.

Acting as activists from this place of lack of responsibility for our own small worlds, we might make some difference at the level of laws (and indeed, that campaign I worked on years ago was a major contributor to passing Michigan's Polluter Pay Bill) *but it won't fundamentally alter the dynamics that set up the problem in the first place.* A company forced to answer to an outside standard of cleanup is far different from a company that is internally motivated to be responsible. Just like those companies, I could have decided to start taking care of myself before the metaphorical frying pan hit me over the head. But I didn't. I passed out and spent days recuperating; they too opted to not be responsible for their messes, and had a law forced down their throats. And my guess is that they were just as resentful of that law as I was of my body giving out on me.

Besides being hypocritical (which you might think you can live with) there is a second, more insidious reason for activists to change how we are doing things. When we do not embody an internally motivated responsibility, the only victory we are ever going to have is one in which we create an "enemy." Once we have labeled someone an enemy, we have created a hostile context for them to operate within. In this dynamic, we have stacked the deck so that it is extremely difficult for them to actually get the point of being responsible – their attention is more often than not on not being villainized (thus the modern tactic of "green washing").

Think about what it feels like in your own life when someone has decided you are the "bad guy." Usually, by that point, there isn't much room for working together amicably – their label of you has predetermined how cooperative your relationship can be. This is not simply a "dynamic between activists and corporations"; this creation of enemies is *our creation as activists* – no one considers themselves an "enemy" until someone labels them that way.

Companies subjected to laws that came out of this dynamic may follow the letter of the law, but they will rarely have any motivation for aligning with the intention behind it. By choosing to view corporations as the enemy of the earth, we are literally creating a role for them to play. What's remarkable to me is that we are shocked when they play it!

With this antagonistic setup, companies may well be motivated to try to get away with more of what we don't want, simply because they have already been labeled that way. There is, after all, no real motivation for cleaning up your act if someone in your life already has you firmly labeled in some way. It's the old psychology of, "Well, I might as well do what I'm being accused of since I seem to be being punished for it anyway." It may seem petty and childish on some level, but that is how most of us respond to being labeled in some negative way or being told what to do.

For activists to not take into account this human tendency is folly on our part. It's an example of refusing to know the nature of ourselves.

Ultimately, we fail even if we win. A campaign that is "successful" in its surface level goal, but uses the tactic of creating an enemy in the process has just added another building block to the precise set of dynamics we are trying to undo. I don't believe that any of us really want a society in which corporate interests and environmental interests are at odds. But I also don't believe that this dynamic will change until we are willing to stop reinforcing it. What this means first and foremost, is to drop the "enemy" label.

To unapologetically use a spiritual phrase: What you resist persists.

The first step to having less of what we are resisting in the world is to stop resisting it within ourselves. When we can own up to the fact that we do things we don't ideally want to be doing, we can change those things. And to do so with gentleness and compassion for ourselves (sometimes making changes DOES feel hard, and does require some real effort) allows us to later have compassion for others going through a similar process—regardless of whether those "others" are our sister, our city council or a corporation.

This is very different than blame. Blame says there is something wrong with us. In blame, there is no such thing as a mistake; there is very little room to shift our perspective. Things that we see in others are interpreted as indicating a flawed nature or bad intent. We create enemies because we are looking for someone to blame.

The standard resist/persist dynamic that still characterizes the majority of activist efforts is far different than some of the work that's been done out West where ranchers and environmentalists are starting to get together and talk. Instead of demonizing "the enemy" and resisting their actions and beliefs, they are working on humanizing each other, sharing the stories of their lives, and starting to work together for common goals. Those conversations have not always been easy and rosy, but they represent an important beginning to undo our knee-jerk labeling of each other. This approach is easy to call "sleeping with the enemy" but it is actually an approach that has simply left to the side a belief in enemies, and it appears to be slowly making a lasting impact. Better still, some of the best work in land reclamation in New Mexico is being done by an old time rancher. He has, for practical reasons of his own, refused to play one side of the dichotomy, and has found that he can have success at both ranching and being a responsible steward of the land.

So this brings me back to the point about *growing into* responsibility, and growing into an ability to address larger and larger domains of responsibility. First, we need to address our own acts and decisions, based on our own ethical standards. If contributing to the destruction of the earth is not ethical in your book, then start acting on your own ethics. Begin by getting honest about what you are doing right now that violates that ethical standard[18]. When you have successfully been able to make some changes, then you can enroll others in your immediate circle—maybe family or friends, and offer to them an opportunity to become more aligned with *their own* ethics in this area.

Please note the phrasing: you help others align *their own lives with their own ethics*—not your ethics. The ethics may be similar, and it is effective activism to empower those with ethics that are aligned

---

[18] Warning: this is not a process for people who like life to be black and white, or people who are really tied to appearances. The reality for most of us is that the deeper we go into aligning our lives with our ethics, the more things can look complex—at least from the outside. For instance, part of my work in the world is as a facilitator for groups. My work isn't all local at this point (though I am moving toward that as my goal.) So I travel. The work is aligned with my deepest values, and burning gas isn't. So, what to do? I take the train more than ever, and I bought a Toyota Prius hybrid. And I let myself sleep at night. The internal experience is simpler, but it probably looks pretty wonky from the outside.

with yours, but it is a very different thing from attempting to impose your ethics upon another person.

At this point, you'll be able to make that as an offer of real, knowledgeable support, not as a judgment, because you know what it takes to make those decisions to change and act upon them. You can be both compassionate and practical. Once you've been able to inspire and support a few others, you can move on to a larger domain — perhaps a neighborhood association or business setting. Then move on to the city or county level, eventually working your way up. But it all starts with your own personal cleanup.

Anything else besides this gradual building of capacity is not only ineffective, it is dishonest. This is because *we don't really know a path until we have walked it for ourselves.*

And at every step, we expand our capacity to be responsible — to have a role in a larger and larger domain. This version of responsibility is not the typical one of heaviness and obligation; it is responsibility born of self-awareness and a willingness to see ourselves as having an important contribution to make to our world.

What happens when we don't do this? When we don't allow ourselves to be in a gradual process? What happens when we fake it and try to claim we are ready for a level of responsibility we aren't actually ready for?

Think about this in terms of economics. If you aren't yet at a place where you can pay the rent on a small studio apartment, or a room in a house, would any sane person commit to buying a half million-dollar home? Or think about the challenges that single teen mothers face. They may rise to the challenge of parenting, but chances are it is going to be a difficult experience because they haven't yet had the opportunity to fully develop responsibility for themselves as adults. The first step has been skipped, and they are trying the difficult task of building on a nonexistent or shaky foundation. The same woman ten years later would probably have a completely different experience, simply because she will have given herself the time to develop some sense of self-responsibility before jumping into being responsible for another.

When you haven't yet become responsible for your own ecological practices, trying to get a huge company to be responsible for theirs is a similar pretense. You'd be in over your head if anyone ever asked you how to actually do that, and because that company's needs are at, say, step J and you haven't yet completed step D, you aren't actually in a position to even see it clearly and be of any real assistance in their process.

Identities in Conflict

This personal consciousness stuff can seem overly complex at times, even though the process for sorting it out is relatively simple (get more honest and be more responsible). We have layers of identities interacting with each other, personal needs and wants vying to get met, messy old creations with people in our lives that cloud our ability to simply see them for who they are, transgressions that have us act through veiled shame. Underneath it all, though, I believe we have a core urge to serve others. Our essence is to be noble, honest and transparent, so that we can contribute something of real value to the world around us.

So, how do identities operate? One part of us may say, "I won't participate in damaging the Earth." Another is just trying to get the bills paid, and makes our compromises. Yet another is trying to get and keep the approval of friends and will violate the value of "not damaging the Earth" if it means participating in an event with the gang. When you jumble all of this together, it is no wonder that most of us are inconsistent and moody, and looking for anyone to blame other than ourselves. Unpacking personal consciousness is an act of bravery—and importance—on par with cleaning up a toxic waste dump and reclaiming the sacred land it poisoned.

It is, in fact, a parallel process running on two different levels of existence. Personal consciousness addresses that toxic gook which is closest to home. Environmental activism addresses the collective toxins we've spilled into the earth.

Chapter 4: Motivation: Moving from Facts to Heart

"We have, for the entire history of humanity, been laboring under wrong information about how the world works. There is no reason to think that now is any different. We don't teach children 'facts' at this school; we teach them how to ask their questions, find their own answers, and live with the consequences of those answers."

— Gael Keyes, Principal, The Family School, Albuquerque NM

How do you feel about facts? How do you feel in the presence of someone sharing (or making a point with) a fact? How do you use facts in your life?

I am going to include the "liberal use of facts" in my indictment, and for many this will feel like I am going for the jugular of the scientific world. I am afraid that can't be helped, because while I have tremendous respect for science on many levels, facts are a mixed bag for activists.

Facts are one of the things I consider from the perspective of evaluating things based on their *usefulness*. Usefulness is always tied to a specific goal. In one circumstance, it might be useful to have a good intellectual analysis of something (say in a college class). In another situation, intellectual analyses could get in the way (say when you are having a romantic evening out).

Because intellectualizing is not always useful does not mean it doesn't have inherent value, but it does mean it's best to use some discernment as to when it is useful and when it isn't. If our goal is to be effective activists, then we have to look at the tools we are currently employing to see if they really do serve that goal or not. Questions like, "What purpose does the use of this thing serve?" and "Whatever the intention, how is this actually playing out in our world?" are better barometers for me in how I work with sustainability issues than some supposedly objective measure of "the truth."

We, as a culture, have a tremendous investment in facts and science. For many, it is the thing that distinguishes modern life from the "Dark Ages." We believe that we somehow have a firmer grasp on some immutable reality for having invested ourselves so thoroughly in facts. We have come to confuse sound bites and bits of information—usually taken out of context, because the context takes too long to explain thoroughly—with an actual experience of the physical world. We think we know something about the planet because we can quote some facts about it.

This is, for many people, a place of security. We have gotten a handle on something, we suppose. But basing your life decisions on facts is simply a choice, like any other choice. So I'll start us off by blaspheming the elders in my family and taking facts to task at the get go.

Facts can be valuable things. They can also be dangerous, disempowering weapons. And it isn't just "in the wrong hands" — it can be in the wrong mood, with the wrong agenda, or by the wrong identity[19]. And any one of us can be moody, agenda-laden and operating through an identity that wants to wield some power or convince others that we are right, knowledgeable, etc. Beating people over the head with nuggets of information is a time-honored and deeply disempowering method of "winning" support (and it is so easy when we are invested in facts — which are often seen as black and white — to move into a state of mind that is about winners and losers).

Ramming the facts home until someone agrees with you (sometimes referred to as "debate") is so thoroughly documented as a way of interacting that it even has a name: indoctrination.

I can't stress enough that we do not want indoctrinated people in our movements. Indoctrinate someone for long enough (and with enough heaviness or nasty social consequences for not buying into your indoctrination) and eventually they can't think for themselves. Minds can become cluttered and overwhelmed with information. In a cluttered mind, the pressure to insert a new piece of information and

---

[19] By an identity, I mean some part of yourself that gets expressed for a particular purpose. It could be a role that you play (like "dad" or "teacher") or a major personality trait (like "the joker" or "a control freak".) For a lot of us, our identities are set on automatic, and they come out without us consciously choosing them, or

have it make sense can become too much.

Have you ever argued with someone who seems to constantly change their argument? Then you've seen an overwhelmed mind in action! A person with an overwhelmed mind is not a stable ally; they will sell out the group's perspective without having any real idea that this is what they are doing, simply because they can't hold a cohesive thought under pressure.

Constant arguing can also dull the human spirit. At some point, most of us give up trying to make sense of things, and this moment is a type of submission. That submission is when indoctrination can take hold. From that moment on, a person is easier to influence, but not particularly effective when it comes to original or creative thought.

Indoctrination isn't even particularly practical: what if your goals change or you get a new fact? Then you are going to have a heavy struggle on your hands of undoing one set of indoctrination to try to replace it with another.[20]

If you want to see a tooth and nail fight, threaten someone's hard won indoctrination. We spend hundreds of painful hours in activist circles trying to convince people to stop believing what we once told them to believe. I remember being at a conference for the lesbian/gay/bisexual community years ago, and watching someone come out of one discussion having just been thoroughly convinced

---

without any evaluation of whether they are really useful or not for the situation we are in.

[20] The best experiential exploration of indoctrination and the ability to get past it that I have seen is the Avatar Course. www.avatarepc.com

that being gay was all about genes only to be thoroughly confused in their next workshop by the perspective that it was actually a matter of "everyone being bisexual" and it being easier to express an extreme perspective of "I'm gay" in a social environment that insists on black and white realities. Having just been indoctrinated in one belief, someone else in the same activist community set immediately out to fight with that belief and replace it with another one. What a waste of energy!

When we cave into the demand to have facts on our side, we confuse the actual issues of integrity and human rights to no end. Someone else, after all, is always behaving "more badly" than we are, and here's the facts to back that up. But the scale of how we are out of integrity is actually irrelevant. Being "a little abusive" is still being abusive. If you are married to quantifying everything and making constant comparisons, you are far, far more likely to excuse your own behavior because "the facts say" that something else is far worse than whatever it is that you are personally engaged in. When we play this game, we essentially use facts as a smoke screen to deny personal responsibility, and that is exactly what the planet does not need at this time.

Meanwhile as we are busy debating the facts, the tangible, physical world is floating past, and quite possibly not improving in a direction we like.

When Facts Change

My father, Dr. James Ludwig, tells a story that illustrates another challenge around facts. When DDT[21] was initially introduced in the 1950's, it was hailed as a godsend. Suddenly regions of the world that were overrun with malaria-carrying mosquitoes found some relief. It was, truly, a miracle. People had been dying and suffering in large numbers from simple mosquito bites, and suddenly there was a way to prevent that.

Within short order, however, more information began to come out about the nature of DDT. In one of the quickest turn-arounds in the history of modern science, people who had once hailed its properties were backtracking and insisting that it was actually a devastating chemical that should not be poured into the natural environment. Now the real work began of convincing people that it was more long-term trouble than it was worth. Surely people whose lives had been greatly improved in one quick sweep would argue that their lives benefited more than were damaged. One could hardly expect anything else.

So facts change, and they are time- and perspective-dependent. One minute, DDT is a godsend; the next, it is a human created plague. In some places in the world, it is experienced as a

---

[21] DDT (Dichloro-Diphenyl-Trichloroethane) is an insecticide that has been banned for agricultural use, but is still used in some parts of the tropics to kill malaria-transmitting mosquitoes.

blessing; in others, a curse. Which is true? Both and neither. It is good wisdom to not be too convinced of the absolute rightness of any fact, no matter how true it may seem at the time.

Most honest statisticians will tell you that facts are malleable things. While I am bought into certain overall patterns that are described by facts (and also visible to my own eyes — like the idea that that purplish smoke coming out of the incinerator stacks is probably not something I want to breath) I find myself wary of any particular nuggets or factoid these days. And, like many people, I've grown weary of them, and the push to buy into the favored fact d'jour. Our tendency toward rapid-fire quotes, which supposedly represent the truth, is more of a drain than a useful tool. Facts tell me little of how to live a good life, and give my mind much to torture me with in the wee hours of the morning.

So do we ignore facts? Nope. But I'd strongly encourage finding them a place that they are suited to and not using them where they are not. A good use of facts, for instance, might be for tracking progress or regress on a certain issue. Statistics created ten years apart with the same methodology can give you a sense of a general trend. Are the Great Lakes cleaner than they used to be? Has the ozone layer over Australia thinned any more? Those are benchmarks that can be useful as facts.

I had an awful struggle with the social services office in Michigan when I tried to enroll my son, Jibran, in the state supported medical program. At the time, his father and I had been split up as a couple for several years. He was already living in New Mexico and we were all trying to make it work for our family to still function as a family for Jibran. They were insisting that I needed to report a whole array of information about his dad to them because he was an "absentee father" (the result of which would have been a warrant for his arrest).

It took hours of explanation with various workers to finally get them to understand that he hadn't actually abandoned his child simply because he was living elsewhere. The workers there were so schooled in "the facts" about abandonment that they literally couldn't think outside of that box. Although they were coming from a good intention (making sure that abandoned kids were cared for) the insistence on one size fits all interpretation meant that they couldn't see an exceptional situation when it presented itself. Very few lives fit into neat boxes; insisting on living by statistics means missing out on much of real life.

Creating a belief system that you hang your life and actions on based on today's facts is not my recommended approach to activism. Facts change. Sometimes daily. Facts are spun for maximum benefit to the spinner (i.e. manipulated in order to manipulate). Facts are generated out of the beliefs of the researchers, funders and press, many of whom have their own agendas for playing with facts in the first place, and then used selectively by all sorts of people to convince us of the rightness of what they want to do. Many of us are unaware of just what our beliefs and agendas really are. So the manipulation is often unintentional, and invisible to us[22].

I am not fond of conspiracy theories, but I do think that the liberal use of facts is suspect behavior in anyone, and that it is a far more sane approach to encourage real self-responsibility than it is to encourage endless fact mongering. Just about everyone these days is familiar with the overall state of things; it is a far better use of time, energy and good will to simply get on with the work of becoming more aware and self-responsible than it is to recapitulate facts.

And here's the kicker — if you start exploring your own consciousness, with sincerity, honesty and good intent, you will naturally discover those places where you are less than responsible, be it with money, your kids, your work, your relationships, or the planet, *and you will do this regardless of what facts you do or don't know.* When it comes to examining our own dark corners and changing your own behavior, that motivation comes not from the head but from the heart.

You have to *care* to do the work that I am suggesting. You have to be able to empathize with others to get real about the impact of your own actions. And these things — care and empathy — happen in the heart, not the head. Facts move us in the opposite direction — toward intellectual analysis and debate, with its tendency toward making each other wrong. You can't simultaneously care about someone and make them wrong.

---

[22] This can actually be more dangerous than someone with a knowing, deliberately hurtful agenda, because the person's lack of awareness is a

The bottom line is that facts don't matter *unless* people have some personal motivation for acting on them, and that they are best used lightly when dealing with humans (who, by the nature of our egos, will attempt to worm our way out of being responsible, given any small doorway out.) Don't cater to the ego; instead, appeal to our equally powerful innate sense of doing right in the world. Until we move out of a mode where we are leading with the facts, and leading with the gloom and doom routine, we will be contributing to the debilitation of that which we love.

From Argument to Bridge Building

There are multiple different basic ways we can interact with the world. If you could see these as layers that represent different ways of being, facts live in a similar spectrum to opinions and assessments. While I want to be clear that I see value in all of these things, I believe that this domain is the domain of divisiveness. People argue about facts, opinions and assessments. More and more, I am seeing the most effective dialogues happening in the arena that lives at a level below the fact level—that of people telling their personal stories. Stories and personal vulnerability about how they have affected us as real people—this is the level at which bridge building and connection can take place, and this is where creative, out-of-the-

whole other layer of what needs to get addressed before things can change, and people's willingness to look at their own motivations varies widely.

box solutions can emerge.

I was privileged to be one of ten facilitators who worked with a Hate Crimes dialogue in Santa Fe, New Mexico in the summer of 2006. The dialogue was set up for and financed by the city, and a wonderful group called the Community Dialogues Network was brought in to facilitate it. The small group that I worked with had two young women of color who were gay community activists, and also had two seasoned police officers in it. One of the young women took to heart my request that we listen to each other's stories and really be open to hearing the humanity in each other. Over the course of one hour, she reached out repeatedly to one of the officers while he described his own experiences as someone who is targeted for violence just because of who he is—just like the members of the gay community—and about his experience of being shot on the job.

She finally looked across the circle and asked him the question, "What happens to police officers when something goes wrong on the street?" His response was, "If they don't have good support at home, they drink. Sometimes, they become that bad cop you have talked about meeting on the street."

There was a moment of hushed, almost reverent silence after this statement. His vulnerability, and her willingness to hear and accept it, changed the whole nature of the conversation. As we continued into the next phase of the dialogue, talking about what we could do to make the streets safer for everyone, our group found ourselves all reaching out to the officers and looking at what we could do to empower these folks whose job it was to keep the streets safe.

75

"How can we support the emotional health of the police?" was the unlikely question we found ourselves asking as the result of talking about hate crimes.

There was magic in that dialogue—the magic that only comes from listening to stories, and not falling into the temptation to argue about it all. No "fact" could have created that moment.

Chapter 5: Victims, Abusers and the Messy In-Between

Are we abusing the planet? Do we feel like victims of the planet's limited "nature," afraid of the outcome and powerless to act in this big, big domain? It's a fair bet that we could answer yes to both.

So, what's going on here? Are we abusers or victims?

Abuse and victimhood are two sides of the same coin. When you abuse in one arena, you open yourself to feeling like a victim, either in that same arena, or another. It is the self's way of trying to bring balance into our lives and consciousness. It is as if our higher selves are saying to us, "See how it feels to be a victim—get some compassion and stop abusing..." When we are careless and callous, we often find ourselves feeling not cared for and disregarded.

When it comes to the planet, we are generally participating in both sides of this consciousness simultaneously. Powerlessness comes from feeling small in the face of the seemingly insurmountable challenges. This leads to victim consciousness, which is one big part of why we are ineffective (this is the "shame" side of the equation.). Ironically, those same feelings contribute to our ongoing abuse of the planet: when one feels like a victim, the temporary antidote to those feelings is doing something that makes us feel powerful. The urge to make some ripple in the world, affect *something*, can cause us to act in a manner that is less than noble. This is at the heart of abuse. The tangible results of our abuse are slowly piling up, in the form of toxic waste, trash, rising CO_2 levels, etc. And this is just creating more and more evidence for our feelings of victimhood. It's a vicious cycle!

Whatever it may look like on the surface, the source of these *feelings* of victimhood is not the mounting ecological problems. Rather, it is our consciousness and the closely linked state of our own integrity. Take a moment now and remember how you feel when you know you have behaved badly toward someone in your life. Just pause here for a moment and feel that feeling. Maybe you yelled at someone who didn't really deserve it. Maybe you shut someone out, or abandoned someone on a project you had committed to doing with them.

I'd submit that it isn't that *person* who is the source of your feelings of discomfort or guilt (though the feelings may be triggered by their presence) but rather the prodding of your own conscience. The remedy is often a sincere apology and an effort to make up any damage done. Then, suddenly, you feel more comfortable with them again. Before that happens, though, it's easy to interpret bad feelings in a way that sure seems like you are the victim; you just feel bad.

The same is true for how you behave with regard to the planet. Integrity is measured by our willingness to see, own and repair the damage we are responsible for in the world. When a person is in integrity, they no longer feel like a victim. Instead, they see in front of them practical steps to be taken to correct a wrong in the world. Their attention is freed up from guilt and justification and available to act. This is an effective activist.

By taking responsibility for our actions, we do two things at once. First, we close those loopholes in our lives that allow the abuser/victim consciousness to creep in and disempower us as individuals. At the same time, we move our actions further away from contributing to the physical damage of the planet. Only by doing both of these things can we truly contribute to the health of the planet, because *consciousness and the physical plane are inseparable.*

Integrity, Wholeness and Effectiveness

I use the word integrity deliberately. Integrity is commonly understood to mean things like honesty, aligned words and actions, and having some attention on how your actions affect others. While all of these meanings of the word are in play here, the word integrity also comes from the same roots as "integrated" and "integration."

Integrity implies a wholeness, an easy alignment of the different parts of the self. Inherent in this wholeness is a lack of separation (either internally with all parts of your life or self working together harmoniously, or externally with relation to others and, particularly in this case, the planet.) What I am suggesting is a version of personal integrity that includes both the more common associations with the word, as well as real integration. This includes resolving your victim/abuser consciousness, by accepting that you've played both of those roles and are committed to stop. What can follow is playing a new game in which your actions reflect a co-creative, connected relationship with the planet.

As I've said before, this is really the opposite of the "denial" method of dealing with the planet, the "everything's OK with what we are doing, and those liberals are just scaring you" thing. What I am talking about sidesteps the political realm, which is so enmeshed in the particulars of time and place and personalities, and fed by dramatic displays. I am sidestepping the political, not because it doesn't have any value, but because I believe this realm is not where the bulk of our attention is best invested at this time. What I am suggesting is a transcendent journey into the more spiritual realms of life. It is a place where connection and self-responsibility are the tools that move us ahead on our development, and make for a vibrant, creative life.

This is the integration between the spirit and the physical, a making sacred and whole these two arenas of life. It is one of the great spiritual journeys of our time, a modern equivalent of the Bodhisattva's path to be self-responsible and enlightened, yet still choose full engagement with the physical plane — and with other humans. In this case the work extends beyond humanity and into selfless service to the planet itself. This is not an ungrounded, stereotypically "new agey" attempt to escape, nor is it something available to a chosen few who have some miraculous set of traits that make them special. It is non-exclusive, available to everyone willing to do the work of being responsible.

Real self-responsibility is the most deeply practical contribution we could make to anything we truly care about, *and anyone can do it.*

Now the word "responsible" is a big button for a lot of folks. It sounds heavy, and usually comes on the tail end of a specific list of "shoulds." It is closely linked with guilt in most circles. This is not the type and feel of responsibility that I am talking about.

Let me draw a distinction: Guilt is a very effective short-term motivator for change, which ultimately results in nothing (or sometimes results in backtracking). Guilt is often referenced to what someone else believes you should be doing (thus the term "guilt-tripping"). Responsibility, on the other hand, is a long-term energy-producing activity that is closely linked to your own ethical structure. Real responsibility is motivated by an internal sense of what is right and appropriate; it requires having some real connection with your own values.

The primary benefit we get from this level of responsibility is the attention that is freed up by not playing games. When you are not invested in the victim/abuser dynamic, and can't be drawn into the fear, blame or guilt that it engenders, you have the attention to act on behalf of your own deepest values. You are able to simply be present with the information available about the state of the world, see it clearly, and act on it appropriately. There are no hours of agonizing, nor is energy required to actively ignore information, or spiral into feeling overwhelmed.

Responsibility of this sort is met with relief, rather than dread.

Chapter 6: Enlightened Eco-Activism

"Following another's path leads to who they are, not who you are."[23]

— From *Love Precious Humanity*, Harry Palmer

E veryone wants to feel heard. Whole personal growth and communication practices are based on helping people really hear each other[24]. One important aspect of this for activists to develop is an ability to meet people where they are. Speak their language. Walk in their shoes. All that good stuff. This creates a bridge for people where they can see themselves shifting from where they are right now into the next step in their own evolution.

Being able to see some aspect of what the world needs (in

---

[23] *Love Precious Humanity*, quotes by Harry Palmer/edited by Kayt Kennedy, 1999.
[24] Marshall Rosenberg's Non-Violent Communication technique is an excellent example of this, and well worth checking out.

other words, being a visionary) is only one step in effective activism. You also need to be able to facilitate people actually moving their lives toward that vision, by helping them understand what is valuable *for them* in that vision and then find the internal strength to move toward your vision. This is about inspiring people to find their own right path, not indoctrinating them to follow you in yours. But in order to do it effectively, you have to learn to first listen to where they are at.

So meeting people where they are becomes imperative. And we can't do that unless we first are honest about where we are in our own lives. If you aren't practicing what you preach, it will ring hollow. No one can grow or change if they are in pretense about who they are being right now. You can't start where you aren't. Many of the frustrations people have with personal growth come from not being willing to honestly assess where they are at—by a refusal to own their starting place. And no set of personal tools, however powerful, can make a significant dent in consciousness based on this particular denial.

Similarly, no political action can affect a company or governmental agency that is in denial of where they are currently. Gandhi said, "Be the change you wish to see in the world." If we want large, powerful bodies to change their behavior and get out of denial, we need to model that behavior ourselves. Anything else is hypocritical, and diminishes the integrity, and therefore the social power, of our movements.

What I am suggesting could be referred to as enlightened eco-activism. I use the word enlightened because this is about: 1) coming to peace with the overall creation; 2) seeing ourselves as part of it rather than separated from it; and 3) having the ability to view it from the perspective of calm observer instead of an emotional reactive, at-effect-of perspective that encourages victimhood. It is calm, centered, Buddha-like. From this perspective, one can both see clearly and act effectively.

This Buddha-like state requires us to stop projecting the worst of ourselves out there on some other person, corporation or governmental agency. Projection requires that we feel separate from the other; conversely, the space available for projection closes when we can see ourselves as being part of the problem. While humans are particularly creative about coming up with things to project on each other, there are some predictable patterns. The most classic projection we have in the ecological movement is the "corporations are only motivated by money" creation.

Our government and corporations—however much we hate to admit it—are reflections of us. By "us" I mean the big collective "us"—who we are actually being in our own lives. As a relevant example, most families are financially stressed and try to find the easiest, cheapest ways to do everything. And that is exactly what corporate America and most bureaucracies are also doing.

I decided about 10 years ago that I was not going to ask anyone to do something I wasn't personally willing to do. Since making that decision, my personal sense of peace has slowly been going up, and my ability to point fingers has slowly gone down. I have had to step up to the plate in my own life.

Projection is not necessarily a simple thing. I used to think that projection meant that if I am mad at John for doing X specific action, then I needed to look at myself for that same X specific action. And I'd generally get stuck there, and decide that the whole projection thing was just silly, because I couldn't find in myself that specific behavior.

But it's often more subtle than that. If X action is manipulative, and it is bugging me, it may simply be that John is more skilled or obvious at manipulating than I am! It doesn't mean that my version of manipulation isn't there; I might just be sneakier about it. When you are looking at integrity, go broad, and look first at those actions you do, or things you say that simply feel a little off to you; those are the places to start. And if you do catch yourself in a blame game, be willing to go broad and subtle as you are looking for what it is that you do.

Maybe some large corporation has done something that you feel is just obviously morally repugnant—maybe it's child slave labor. You can't even stand to hear about it, it's so awful. Now clearly, you don't have literal child slaves in your home whose sole responsibility is doing your bidding and who are punished by being beaten. But it could be, perhaps, that there are ways that you manipulate people into doing things for you more subtly, using whatever power or influence you over them.

Some examples:

- I don't want to play the heavy with the kids, so I guilt trip my husband into doing it for me, sidestepping my own responsibility as part of the parenting team.

- I'm still mad at my ex for leaving me, so I whine, complain or get angry in order to get my way whenever we have to interact with each other.

- I feel overwhelmed with my three kids, so I butter up my oldest to have her take more responsibility than she is ready for or is appropriate.

All of these things are domination and power tripping, just as surely as blatant acts like child slavery. They are just different degrees of the same power games designed to get someone to do something for you that you don't want to have to do. Any one of them will create a subtle internal pressure within you to get noticed and brought back into integrity. We start to see people outside of us doing horrible things, and more and more attention goes to those acts and those people, as our unconscious (or higher) selves try to send us the message. Instead of just not buying a product we know has a practice involved in its making that we don't want to support, we find ourselves emotionally hooked into it, judgmental and stressed out.

As long as our attention stays "out there" on what others are doing, we don't get the hint and look for a similar set of behaviors inside and we won't be able to clean up our own integrity. Now if our integrity only affected us, this wouldn't be such a big deal. We'd die miserable and that would be that for this lifetime. But because it does affect others, we make a negative contribution to the overall integrity of the world, and those things we criticize grow more intense.

For an activist, nothing could be worse. Every time you attempt to address something in the outside world that reminds you of your own lack of integrity, you get defensive or angry or powerless. You can't actually address things effectively, no matter how sharp your intellect or how learned your perspective. No manner how many dedicated hours you put in, and no matter how much you try to "stay calm" during the conversation, nothing works. The reality is that you aren't really present and available to have a calm conversation, because some part of you is working really hard to keep your own transgressions tucked out of sight and out of mind[25].

Without integrity, it all falls down, eventually. And because of this, we cannot separate our personal lives from our activism. It also means that we are sometimes "inexplicably" drawn to do the work that is closest to where our own lack of integrity lies. This is at the heart of some occasionally really vicious activist moments, where people go for someone's jugular, or drive a boat into a whaling ship, knowing it will kill people. Our integrity is so far out of whack that we have to cover it up by drawing as much attention to the other, so that there isn't any attention on us and what we have done (or are doing).

The adage that we teach what we most need to learn also applies to activism. We also demand of others what we most need to clean up in ourselves.

---

[25] The Avatar mini course on integrity addresses this phenomenon in detail. You can download it at www.avaterepc.com/html/mini-eng.html

So is it possible to do "clean" activism work? Or are we just doomed to not be able to act on anything, or to never be able to trust ourselves?

The answer lies not in what we are doing, but in *how easily* we are able to do it. If it takes effort to not get angry, there's something there to be cleaned up[26]. If you are able to listen to others, even those people who are on the exact opposite side of a question from you, with easy attention and a willingness to really hear them, then you are in a good place to be doing the work you are doing.

Demonizing is a specialized form of projection. When we demonize, we make someone else out to be a monster. We demonize out of fear. The more we feel is at stake, the more tempting it is to demonize. When it comes to the idea that we may just be destroying an entire planet, it sure feels like there is an awful lot at stake!

Here's an anecdote. We are sitting in the living room of my teaching companions Maggie and Zaida. It is the first night of the new Personal Sustainability 101 class, and the seemingly inevitable happened. Instead of keeping the conversation "personal," someone wandered into the "corporations are the problem" perspective and most of the room jumped on the bandwagon. It can be very difficult for us to sustain a personal examination. To their credit, when the students in the class had it pointed out to them that they were angry at corporations for using similar thinking to their own ("I can't afford

---

[26] Please note that I am not talking here about a situation where someone is pointing a gun at you. That is a situation where instincts serve us well. I am talking about a

to be more eco-friendly") they accepted the feedback with thoughtfulness and — for the most part, anyway — grace.

How many of us lobby to willingly pay more taxes for environmental laws to be better enforced? How many of us buy stuff from mega-companies with iffy environmental and social practices simply because it is cheap? How many of us take full responsibility for our waste? I have a couple friends who would probably qualify as pretty squeaky clean in the actions department. But in most cases, their "talk" has the feel of real dogma and anger behind it — doing things to prove someone else wrong, and in order to feel superior.

Is it possible to act in full integrity and speak our truth without blame and dogmatic righteousness coming in to play?

I say yes. But this is the stuff of gradual progress, not sudden conversions. Changing our lives gradually, over a year or five years or fifteen, is a process that is steady, gentler. Gradual change is an alternative to drama and conflict, and for a lot of people this lack of drama is equated with a lack of excitement. The net result is a life that feels more peaceful and is often more effective and fun, but it probably won't make the nightly news.

A friend of mine relates this move away from drama and conflict to her own physical move from New York City to New Mexico. In New York, she was accustomed to constant bustle, noise and billboards — excitement at every turn! When she first came out to New Mexico, she didn't see beauty; she saw **boring**. She suffered, in

---

higher realm of consciousness—the relational arena and acts with a bit more distance to them.

those first months, from a lack of stimulation. After she'd been here for a while, the quiet, more subtle beauty of the desert started to grow on her, and it is now a source of great comfort and pleasure. But in order to appreciate it, she had to stop expecting that level of stimulation, and become open to simpler, calmer, more peaceful pleasures.

Changing ourselves first is a quiet evolution without the stimulation and adrenaline rush of demonizing and making others wrong. An Earth First activist/musician by the name of Dakota Sid has a song that includes the line, "There ain't no real monsters here, except for me and you." We recognize ourselves as the demons and then thoughtfully evaluate our own actions and words, putting into action those changes that we recognize as valuable at the point that we feel a real internal motivation to do so.

So the new piece of environmental activism is more like facilitation or coaching work. You help get people to recognize the projection for what it is—an attempt to avoid personal responsibility. It's not as exciting, perhaps, as going to rallies, or as ego-gratifying as pulling our friends and colleagues into agreement about how horrid something (or someone) is. It won't make the press like eco-sabotage will. The reality is, I'm advocating for a process that, like my friend's first glimpse of New Mexico, might look pretty damn boring from the outside. But it is a path of really creating more responsibility in life[27].

---

[27] The good news is that after a time, being more responsible does start to feel exciting. There's a creativity that goes with being more clear, and personal work can

It is also a path that allows us to see "good guys" in the corporate world who are doing things as well as we are, or maybe even better. It allows us to be fascinated by the companies (such as Ford Motor Company and Nike) that have hired radical green architect William McDonnough to rework huge factories into net positive environmental structures, without then feeling a need for looking for the other skeletons in their closet. Or to be able to applaud Los Alamos Labs (generally cited as one of the biggest baddies in the Southwest) for undertaking a radical redesign of their facilities to be more ecologically friendly. We don't ignore the other aspects of their environmental records, but we are being open to supporting their development, just like we would an imperfect friend, or a spouse with faults.

Corporations are not obligated to be any more ethical than we are.

Think about conversations you have had with friends when you've had difficult feedback to give them. Most people respond better if you include with your criticism an acknowledgment of what they are also doing right or well, or how they have grown recently. There is a now almost stereotypical way of giving feedback that involves sandwiching the tough stuff in between two positives. It has reached stereotypical proportions because it is used a lot; and it is

---

start to feel a bit like an adventure… going hunting for that thing that is throwing me off. It's *interesting*, this consciousness stuff.

used a lot because it works better for most people[28].

One of my dearest friends is a woman who is deeply dedicated to personal work. We are part of an ecovillage group together in Albuquerque, and at one point the group was exploring frustrations about people not following through on their commitments. Rather than blame and complain, we decided to ask the question, "If someone perceives that you aren't doing what you said you would, how can we most effectively give you that feedback?" Her reply, only half-jokingly was, "Sugar-coat it." Now, she might be a little extreme, but I think she was honestly naming what most people really feel—tell me how great I am even while you have to tell me I've screwed up. And she's right—if you lay on the compliments, you can say just about anything to her, and she responds well.

Again, corporations and governments are made up of real people, and those people are just as subject to going defensive on you and not listening as anyone else. It behooves us to see the positives, and acknowledge and celebrate them, because it puts us in a better position to address the uglies.

So, is there ever a place for dramatic displays and

---

[28] My husband, Laird Schaub, is a group process consultant. We have one of our rare professional disagreements about this one, and I want to give his perspective a fair shake. Laird believes that this formula is so overused that most people don't even hear the compliment because they are waiting for the other shoe to drop. My feeling is that there is skill involved with getting to the point where both can land well, and it has a good deal to do with having something sincere to say, rather than making up some BS to feed someone to manipulate them into hearing you. But I think he does have a point. I'd suggest using the sandwich technique, but only when you are really sincere.

confrontation? Maybe. *But the most dramatic confrontation is the one we have with ourselves[29].* And that must come first if we are going to live in a world with real integrity.

There are certainly things happening in the world that are created out of a consciousness that is so far out of touch with real compassion and service to others that it results in truly callous treatment of others, and of the planet. These things can be stood up to in a clean and clear way, but only once we have done the work of standing up to those parts of our own consciousness that are selfish and callous. Once we have returned to compassion for our own selves and felt the struggle to reawaken self-responsible Service to others, we can impact change. Gandhi could stand sure because he had done his own soul-searching first[30].

Before that process happens, we do not "know the enemy" (as the best military strategists recommend) and their own potential struggle well enough to confront it effectively. There is a story about an Indian teacher. A mother brought her child before him and asked him to tell the child to stop eating sugar. He gave her a level look and told her, "Come back in two weeks and I will do this." In two weeks they returned and he did indeed tell the child to stop eating sugar.

---

[29] I've actually had moments of processing that have literally felt like an "ego seizure" was happening-- now that's interesting drama!

[30] In the introduction to *Non-Violent Communication*, by Marshal Rosenberg, Gandhi's grandson, Arun, tells a story of having his grandfather teach him about the more subtle and insidious forms of violence by mapping them out like a family tree. The story has a ring of truth and relevance about it because Gandhi had done his own similar process, finding those small acts of violence in himself first. It is the do-your-own-work first approach.

But the mother was confused. "How come you couldn't have just told him that two weeks ago?" she asked. "Two weeks ago, I was still eating sugar," was the answer.

Before we have done the work ourselves, it is out of integrity to ask someone else to do it.

Our progress (and the results) may not look like Gandhi's, but the key thing is that we are progressing. Celebrating small wins is really important; so is trusting that as long as we are progressing and doing what feels right for us that we are indeed contributing.

Another belief that I have that affects my activism is that we sometimes need to integrate something that is not from this lifetime. I go back and forth between calling this a "past life" and seeing it as simply being connected with a large collective soup of consciousness that we each play roles in. Either way though, it means we are each integrating things that sometimes include balancing out karma; if you've been a victim, you might have to, for instance, experience abuser consciousness in order to heal it.

I don't believe that this means we are obligated to wallow in anything that isn't serving us, nor that we have to play up these less than charming parts of ourselves, but it does mean that we might need to experience something, even for a few moments, that we can't see logically choosing to experience. I also don't believe that we need to do any of this on a really big scale; in fact, if you can experience a more subtle expression of something (like catching yourself putting someone down) then you can integrate it without needing to have it escalate to a larger, more damaging scale.

95

Sometimes, a confrontation needs to happen with someone or a group of someones who will not in this lifetime return to compassion. They need, for their own soul growth, the opportunity to experience real ugliness in their own behavior. This may be because they have been abused previously and have been unable to reach a compassionate place with abusers without being one themselves. This time around, they get a choice: to ignore it, deny it, see it, change because of it, or none of these things. The confrontation may still need to happen, even if we don't get out of it what we think we want. And knowing that they might not change (and that being an abuser is a nasty place to live) we can have more compassion for them even while we are in the midst of the confrontation.

When we take on the role of confronter, we are healing some need in ourselves to experience standing up to tyranny. Tyrant and confronter are two of the roles that can be played, and to some extent life is about experiencing these different roles and finding a balanced response to each one. If you find yourself in one of these roles, it is best to recognize that this is just a *role* you are playing, and not who you are. Play it, experience it, and then decide if it serves you or the planet to continue playing it. But don't be confused: you are not, at your essential being "the confronter"; activists can lose track of this, forgetting that we are bigger than the roles we play. Someone obsessively creating being the confronter is not much fun as a teammate.

The key here is that we have collectively created this mess, and the overall complex of *your* consciousness (and mine and Uncle

Mo's and everyone else's) has held space for this to flourish. In reaction to you, and me, and the rest of the "good, nice" folks, there will be tyrants and abusers, as long as we refuse to see those things in ourselves and refuse to believe that they have anything to do with us. There will continue to be this variety of roles to be played as long as human consciousness is still dis-integrated. In other words, if we keep them separated internally (seeing ourselves as being one way, but not another) then we will experience them separated externally (with some people playing out those nasty, horrible disowned roles while others play their opposite).

In order to reach that Buddha-like state of peace, and Gandhi-like state of effective action, we first have to pass through our own sea of consciousness.

Chapter 7: Calling Ourselves On It

"As disagreeable as it may be to contemplate, the dishonesty I encounter in the world is a reflection of my own pretense. Pretending that I am honest and that others are not doesn't work."

– From *Living Deliberately* , Harry Palmer

What attracts your attention, and really gets to you? Noticing what bug us tells us what personal work we have to do next. It isn't the same as having an easy, strong commitment to doing something. I save water in my house to reuse because I live in the desert. It feels right. It's an easy thing, and I don't find myself getting annoyed if I go to someone's house who doesn't do it. I might notice it, and share some ideas. But I don't get all bent out of shape. Usually, people respond pretty well, but if they don't, I don't lose any sleep over it.

On the other hand, I still get baffled, bewildered and actively pissed off when I think about how we export pesticides to other countries. It is **unbelievable** to me that we are so unconscionably selfish that we will willingly poison their environment and their kids with stuff we won't use in-house!

Can you feel the difference between how I respond to water issues and pesticide issues? And this in spite of the fact that our practices with pesticides are really no more heinous than our waste of water.

There is still work for me to do here, because my attention gets stuck and I'm outraged every time I think about that practice. My conversations about the export of pesticides are rarely effective, because I'm fixated and grumpy and dogmatic and don't want to listen to anyone else's perspective on it... You get the picture. It bugs me. I haven't resolved something inside me that gets triggered when I think about it.

So how would I go about addressing this? I might look at how the practice of exporting toxins is a metaphor for my own life — are there ways I make my nasty stuff someone else's problem, for instance? My personal way of dealing with it is to use a process from Avatar, such as one to uncover transparent (hidden from my sight) beliefs[31].

Here are some other examples of what might bug you, and possible venues to start digging around in your own consciousness for the projections:

---

[31] This exercise, plus about 30 others for exploring consciousness, is in *ReSurfacing*®, by Harry Palmer, 2002. ReSurfacing is a registered trademark of Star's Edge, Inc. You can get a copy by going to www.avatarepc.com

- Corporate irresponsibility? Are there ways that you are less than responsible, be it in your business dealings, or elsewhere? Are there ways that you just want to make money, and not look at the effects in the world or on others of how that money is being made?

- Toxic waste? Are there ways you behave that others experience as toxic? Do you spill nasty emotions on the people around you every time you feel uncomfortable, for instance, radiating anger instead of communicating clearly?

- Landfill problems? (Ooh... trash is a great, richly disgusting metaphor...) What or whom do you disregard and treat as trash? What do you undervalue? Or how do you take the easy way out or act from convenience instead of conscience (the psychological equivalent of TV dinners and fast food)?

The point in doing this work isn't that you'll suddenly have blind eyes to the world's problems. The point is that when you can understand, and compassionately experience the psychology of these problems, you can address them from a calm, compassionate place. You start to be willing to see how the world's problems are, in at least some small way, within your arena of responsibility to correct. And you may find in the course of your explorations that your own ecological behavior improves—you may just have more energy to set up a really good water saving system, or more attention to shop the way you want to when you go to the store.

PASSION AS BIG AS A PLANET

There are both programs and perspectives that can help in your exploration of integrity. The most effective of these programs emphasize simple honesty and a willingness to stop projecting onto others (be they individual people, corporations, cultures, social groups, maybe even the whole planet). I can personally recommend Avatar and Non-Violent Communication because I have worked with them, and they have never failed me when I've been willing to get honest. I'm certain there are other good programs out there, and I've included a short list of things that come recommended by people I trust in the first Appendix.

The other line of questioning for yourself that can be invaluable is looking at what is cultural training, and what is real human need. For instance, many things that Americans take as assumed needs (the size of our homes, our overwhelming dependency on cars, the right to be entertained almost constantly) don't represent real needs, and may actually in some cases run counter to getting your more real needs met. For instance, that extra square footage in our homes costs money, which takes most of us time to earn. That time might better be spent with family or friends.

I realized a while back that I was hanging on to certain things simply because I had become accustomed to them. Hopping in the car whenever I need something, for instance, or buying the easy packaging option. I was holding myself back from making certain shifts in my life simply because I didn't really know, in real time and space, what a different life would look like. It's a lack of imagination, really, that holds us back from making certain leaps in our lives. Now, we could blame that on being a TV generation, but frankly it's our own choice to stay unimaginative and unwilling to try that affects our adult behavior more than anything about our upbringing or culture.

When I get out of the small bubble of my personal life, and stretch beyond the common bubbles of how most people around me live, I can see that many people in the world (and some even in my own neighborhood) are not sharing these same assumptions. They aren't accustomed to these same things. It is possible to be human, be happy, be fed and clothed and enjoy myself without these assumptions. They are cultural, and as such they have a limit to their viability and usefulness and "standard practice." So, I've started walking more, using less packaging, and just slowing down.

Is it possible for us to, in a moment of will and vision and commitment, say, "This is how I've lived my life; and from here on out, this new way is how I will live my life"? Sometimes we do this when life seems to have presented us something earth shattering... the death of a loved one, a house fire, a sudden inheritance, a revelatory experience that shifts our perspective. Something happens, and we find that we are forced into changing by that event.

What would it take to give ourselves permission to have this type of shift be internally motivated, to just decide? Would it actually be kinder to ourselves than having change happen via these earth-shattering moments? Life hands us tragedies when we aren't deciding to change without them[32]. Deaths and changes will still happen, but

---

[32] I think of these events as the result of the "Cosmic Frying Pan" phenomenon. Life hands us opportunities to change, and they start out small—a little tap applied to the

they can't shake you out of a stupor if you aren't in one in the first place; they can't rock your world if your world is based on a solid foundation.

And there is such a thing as sustainable rates of personal change. Sustainability isn't just about changing our lives, or how we live them, it is also about altering things at a pace that allows us to keep up with the changes and integrate them easily so they can be continued without stress and strain. We'll explore sustainable rates of change more at the end of the book. For now, suffice it to say that if you don't choose a slow, steady, sustainable change, life will hand you something that necessitates it being more dramatic and painful.

The Power of Getting Real

One of the organizations The Sustain Ability Trust has taught classes with is Habitat for Humanity[33]. We talked ahead of time of the challenge of being an essentially white, middle class group (with the exception of Zaida Amaral, our Brazilian Co-Director) going into a room of mostly poor and working class people of color. We wanted to find a way to be real without being condescending, to meet people

---

head. Gradually, the hit gets bigger, with a little more momentum to it, until one day it's a full blast with a large cast iron frying pan. That's when we have a tragedy. But it's preventable, see? You can tune into the little taps on the head...

[33] Habitat for Humanity is a very cool organization. They work with low-income families to co-create affordable home ownership. Clients actively participate in building their homes, in a model that was, incidentally, developed in an intentional community called Koinonia.

where they were at, without assuming anything ahead of time about where they might be at, based on our perceptions of race and class. And still, we were being brought in explicitly to offer a different perspective on certain lifestyle choices that the Habitat staff thought would be helpful for them, some of which flew in the face of not only their cultural assumptions, but our own. It was a tricky moment for us.

Before we went into the workshop, we made a commitment to be totally real with our clients about our own personal lives and what we were and weren't doing. We wanted to be particularly transparent about those suggestions we were making for things that could be done in their homes to be more ecologically sustainable that we had not personally done for whatever reason. The relief in the room as we each admitted to not being perfect was palpable. By being real and human and imperfect, we were able to open a door for us to be people together on a journey, and start bridging the gaps that have often plagued environmentalists in their work with diverse populations.

People have come to expect judgment and preaching from environmentalists. What people are longing for instead is an honest ownership that we are all in this together, learning and improving, and yes, making our own compromises on the way. We can pretend, but then what we create is a world of pretense, and chances are (human susceptibility to projection being what it is) we will find ourselves noticing all the ways that others are less than honest.

The worst part of this is that we wrap ourselves into a judgment that sucks our energy away from being able to make

105

changes in our lives that more accurately reflect our own most deeply held values.

I spend time in a project in northeastern Missouri called Dancing Rabbit Ecovillage[34]. Dancing Rabbit is one of the leading grassroots projects in the US for doing the daily work of discovering what it means to be an ecologically responsible human. It is an incredible group of committed folks, and the project has been well thought out and well developed.

I regularly run myself through an ecological footprint calculator[35] just to keep it real about how I am doing ecologically. A few years back, when I was living in Michigan, my footprint was running about a 5.7. When I was last at Dancing Rabbit, I ran myself through based on how I was living then, and it came out to about a 2.6. Now, some people at Dancing Rabbit are doing better than that, but very few folks in the US have actually consistently achieved a 2 or less. Later, when living in a co-op house in Albuquerque, I score around a 4.8 (the biggest bugaboo then being that I was flying more regularly than before).

The reality is that we are all still learning, and that the concept of overall sustainable lifestyles is still relatively new and under development. So here I am, writing a book about sustainability, and

---

[34] www.dancingrabbit.org

[35] The numbers quoted above are from the unfortunately now-defunct website www.ecovoyageurs.com, out of Canada, and are measure in hectares. You'd have to come in at less than 2 to be considered sustainable, and the average American is running around 10.3. There are a number of other EF calculators online, however, and they are lots of fun to play with (at least as an eco-geek would define "fun").

it's a goal I have yet to achieve in my own life.

The other thing that I find interesting about my own shifting numbers is the confirmation that context and community matter. The reality is that "I" don't have a fixed creation of how sustainably I am living, and from that place, it is very slippery ground to be critical. For corporations as well, being located in California, for instance, will be different than being located in Nebraska. The laws and expectations of the community they are in vary, as do the support services available to companies to actually help them do things better.

I had been a vegetarian for 3 1/2 years when I got pregnant with my second child. About two months into the pregnancy, I was suddenly on a "vegetarian plus beef and occasional gyros" diet. Less sustainable by the numbers, but more authentic for what I needed at the time.

This brings me back around to one of my main soapboxes: personal responsibility. You can start with those things that are truly, undeniably, your own responsibility. The health of your own body, how you make your income, your integrity, your personal space, what you do with your own trash, what and how much you drive. These are things that, if you are willing perhaps to endure some embarrassment and conversation, you nonetheless don't have to explain it to anyone else, or consult anyone else about. They are yours, you are responsible for them, and the ability to act in these areas is yours and yours alone.

Any power to decide about these things that you've given away can be gently reclaimed, and that in and of itself will be a gift to the world.

You may find, painfully perhaps, that starting to shift your personal sphere reveals those places in your most intimate relationships where alignment is not a simple, easy thing. Sometimes, we have let a spouse decide what we eat, for instance, when our own values point to different answers. Thus begins your first opportunity for compassion, optimism and communication in action.

Chapter 8: Structural Integrity

Structures, including our routines, are those creations that serve a goal well enough that we decide to give them a life of their own. We create them for a purpose. Structures and systems are just habits we have put on automatic—like brushing our teeth when we wake up. Somebody drilled into our heads as kids that brushing our teeth was a way to meet the goal of still having teeth when we are 40, so we created a system, a little mini system called a routine, to align with that goal. And now we don't have to decide every morning if we will brush our teeth, we don't have to review the reasoning and argue with ourselves about the benefits of teeth brushing. We just do it.

Systems of all sorts are like this—it's a decision, based on sound reasoning at some time, to meet some goal, and it has been put onto automatic. There is no difference, on a fundamental level between the "habit" of teeth brushing and the "system" of welfare. Both were debated, a solution was figured out based on the best available information at the time, and the system was stuck in place and is now on automatic. The system is now there in place of the original reasoning, holding place for the fulfillment of some goal, and continually directing energy toward the goal, as it was envisioned at the time it was set up.

Challenging or changing a system requires some major rethinking of what was once a good idea. It also requires a willingness to change the direction of the energy that is feeding that system. This change can't simply take the form of resistance, however. Resistance has a tendency to stick things in place. Push two fists together, and see how quickly they come to a stand still. This is the activist equivalent of resisting The System.

Once systems are in place, we have a tendency to forget that we were the ones that created them in the first place, and that we are the ones that continue to give them life. "You can't fight the system" is an attitude that empowers the structure above the structure makers. And the truth is, you can't fight a system — even if fighting would be the recommended method for change — it was put there to be the steady space holder of some status quo that was serving some goal, and it is doing its job by being self-maintaining.

If we forget that we create them in the first place, we can become trapped in a system and feel powerless. It's the difference between seeing ourselves trapped within something that isn't working versus seeing ourselves as a creator of that thing, with at least one foot outside of it.

The best thing to do in light of a structure you are

experiencing as oppressive is to 1) assist our decision-makers in drawing a distinction between the systems and the system makers; 2) create a new goal (in other words, get clear about what would best serve us next); and 3) cultivate new systems that support that new goal. These new systems may or may not be empowered by the same decision-makers who put the old one in place; in other words, a creative solution can be for a group of people to decide to start meeting a need that we feel the government is inadequate at meeting.

As goals change, our systems will change with them simply because they will stop being fed creating energy and just crumble — again, so long as we are not applying resistance to them. And often when a big system starts to fall apart, it is because ambivalence about it has entered the picture, or it was built on top of ambivalence in the first place[36].

It would be better, of course, if we could recognize old systems for what they are — historical relics from a past consciousness — and let them go when they stop being effective, or when the goals change. We hang on to things often because we are afraid of the disorder and unknown involved with wiping a slate clean. We also generally forget that we were the ones who created them in the first place. Letting go of a "system" that operates on the

---

[36] Over the past ten years, I have slowly become an advocate for consensus-based decision-making, largely because of this ambivalence factor. With the version of democracy we use—voting on things-- we have invested ourselves in a system with winners and losers. And the losers don't have a lot of motivation for really getting behind the winning proposal or candidate—they become a source of ambivalence or even hostility almost as soon as the decision is enacted. Consensus building,

scale of the United States would likely create quite a bit of chaos and unknown. And while we can hardly blame each other for that fear, it is not an empowered (or empowering) stance.

Just as consciousness evolves, so do political systems. While our leaders are more than willing to see this when analyzing other countries (some of whom are deemed to be "ready for" democracy, while others aren't) we have a collective blind spot when it comes to analyzing our own evolution. Is there perhaps a next step for us as well, one that may seem just as radical now as democratic voting did in the early history of America? I think there is, and it is system that has been slowly developing in small communities and organizations for many years, including in Quaker communities. It is called consensus[37].

At one time, decision-making was reserved only for the very elite (i.e. kings and queens) with money, power and education, and more often than not a blood tie to the last monarch. The earliest representative governments continued in this vein. Democracy is the idea that regular people are intelligent enough to have a voice in their own lives, and that they deserve that voice. Slowly during the history

---

however much time it may take, is far better than a voting system that results in a winner and loser.

[37] Consensus is often understood to mean that everyone agrees about everything. This is NOT what I mean. Consensus—functional consensus, anyway—is a process by which each person is heard and a proposal is created taking into account everyone's perspective. It is labor-intensive up front, but the payoff in strong buy-in from all parties is huge—and there is no more building systems on top of ambivalence. The result is implementation of a new plan with a minimal amount of resistance (or none).

of the US, we have added people in to the category of those we entrust with power to help decide, and the constitutional amendments that have given different groups the right to vote are all steps in our evolution. We are now operating with a one-person one-vote system, with a relatively broad definition of "person."

This was, and still is, a major revelation in how politics work.

This is the gift and essence of democracy. We have, however, arrived at a place where there are major rifts in the country, caused (or reinforced) by the inherent win-lose nature of voting. The essence of democracy has gotten lost in the implementation. I like these two definitions of democracy: "The common people, esp. as the primary source of political power" and "the principles of equality and respect for the individual within a community."[38]

I believe that consensus is actually a fulfillment of the principles and values of democracy, because it has inherent in it this respect for the voices of the individual in the community. Each time we vote we have losers, losers whose voices are not held and respected by our decision. Oddly enough, voting — which has come to be thought of almost synonymously with democracy — is actually anti-democratic. Rather than a departure from democracy, I see us evolving into consensus as the long-sought-for fulfillment of a fundamental principle of our country.

In the course of our evolution, there have always been doubts and fears about the next steps. Some people doubted, for instance,

---

[38] *The American Heritage Dictionary*, 1991. Houghton Mifflin Company.

that non-whites and women were intelligent enough to decide political issues. For most of us, these doubts now seem ridiculous. There are doubts now about our ability to really listen to each other at the level that consensus requires. There are *always* doubts about the next evolutionary step. That's just part of the process, and it shouldn't stop us from moving ahead.

For those who will find the idea of moving on from the voting system to be unpatriotic at best (sacrilegious at worst) let me just say that to cling to a system simply out of loyalty is not honoring the originators of that system as important contributors *to our evolution*. It is, in fact, a desecration of them in spirit, because innovators are not generally people who tolerate not moving forward. Benjamin Franklin advocated for a revolution every so often in order to keep a society alive and vibrant. He understood something of how systems need to be reinvented as consciousness changes.

Democracy is a gift to the evolution of humanity; in order to be honored as such, we need to return to the roots of it. I believe we can best do this by beginning to incorporate consensus into our decision-making[39]. It is simple sentimentality to keep in place a system that no longer serves. Evolution happens because you can honor the past without letting it stop you from moving into the

---

[39] In New Mexico, we have an organization called New Mexico First. For the past 20 years, they have conducted "Town Halls" which are basically policy exploration forums, bringing together a (supposedly) representative slice of the New Mexico population and spending two days coming up with a policy statement that is then presented to the requesting organization. Often, that organization is our state legislature. While what they do is not, quite, consensus as I define it, it is a great

future. If we are willing to see with clear eyes, it may be that we can use the best of our long-used systems and consensus in a way that begins moving us toward being a more compassionate, listening-based culture.

Every founder of every movement or project faces the same challenge at some point: to be able to gracefully encourage the dismantlement of our own creations—those systems we created that made it possible to get going and keep going at the time we needed a lot of creative energy to create a new goal. We get attached to our systems because they are familiar or easy, or simply because our ego enjoys having things around that we invented. And while there's nothing wrong with setting up our lives for ease, we must be willing to not become slaves to the system, and allow ourselves to creatively re-invent the systems of our lives as our goals and needs change. The best leadership knows when to graciously get out of the way and let the new step happen (even better is when a leader will then be part of revisioning).

Moving toward consensus will be a process. What I see as the next step in the process is for voting to not be an unquestioned default. Voting can be one system of several, each of which can be utilized where most appropriate to meet the goal of our collective evolution. There are places where hierarchy can serve (i.e. in situations where a manager is needed). There are places where voting has yet to exhaust its usefulness (for instance, in a more sophisticated

---

example of the next, middle step I am referring to that can start a cultural segue out of voting and toward consensus.

election system that allows for run-offs or percentage-based multiple party winners).

Then there are places where consensus could already begin to meet our social and political needs by allowing more depth to the process, and more voices to be really accounted for (such as local town meetings where good proposals can be developed, and for smaller citizen-based groups that are not relying on government to get their needs met.)

Lest we limit the capacity of consensus at the outset, know that there are people who are working on adapting consensus for groups in the thousands. A few years ago, I was in the room with consensus facilitator and teacher CT Butler, for example, when he described his vision of a 100,000-person city using consensus for decision-making. Representative consensus is already being explored in multiple contexts, and I look forward to seeing what they yield.

The Challenge of Scale

In order to have integrity, a structure must be responsive to the real needs of the real people it is designed to serve. "Structural integrity" is an engineering term that means that a material or a building can meet the physical demands inherent in its intended use.

What our system lacks is the political equivalent of structural integrity. I believe that with the materials we have to work with — chiefly a whole lot of people, many varied regions with different needs, and voting with representative democracy for most major decisions — we cannot successfully build a structure that can meet real peoples real needs as a nation. The system, as it currently stands, isn't leaving people feeling heard. It's not an inherent fault of the system — it is trying to use a "material" to meet a need it isn't built for. Like too small beams in a too big roof; eventually it caves in. You can make the beams bigger, or shrink the roof it is trying to serve, but the current mismatch simply won't work.

The biggest challenge we face right now politically isn't divisiveness, it is *scale*. We have created a government that is so large and has such huge responsibilities that it must, of necessity, create behemoth structures in order to get anything at all done. It takes such incredible energy (time, money and creativity) to create these structures in the first place that once they are finally in place, there is tremendous attachment to them among the people who invested that time, money and creativity in them (or who align themselves with the memories of those founders and creative workers).

Unfortunately it takes so long to get the things up and running when we are working on this scale that they are almost always in the historical relic category by the time we work the kinks out and they are functional. Only a system that is human scale will work in the long run and be flexible enough to change as goals change, or be easily dismantled when really big goals change. While there certainly may be corruption in our government, the larger problem is that we are still not willing to let go of our big huge system, and the pride of place of being the major world power. I have a hard time imagining

117

people who could competently (let alone ethically) run a system as large as the one we have.

One of the most refreshing things for me being in India in 2003 was being surrounded by a majority of people who could care less about being in charge of the world. And it was profound to me how palpable that was when I returned — all the subtle ways (both positive and negative) that we as Americans seem invested in that identity, how our patriotism is tied into everything, from marketing ploys to our relatively cheap food and gas supplies.

We are still empowering the system instead of empowering the system makers. And by empowering huge, slow moving systems, we condemn our growth as a culture to match that speed. And I hate to break the news to the folks who are heavily attached to our current system, but human evolution is calling for something right now that moves a hell of a lot more quickly than the US government could possibly keep up with — *not because it is bad or the people within it are corrupt* but simply because the bigger the ship is, the more time and energy it takes to change direction.

I said earlier that the biggest problem we face politically is not divisiveness; yet the problem with divisiveness is not unrelated. Divisiveness (and again, I think this is an inherent fault with voting systems) makes it hard to trust each other. And without trust, it becomes harder and harder to let go of an old system (a known) even one that is oppressive or sluggish, or not aligned with Service to the people and the planet, because *our lack of trust of each other makes living through the unknown of recreating something that much scarier.*

118

Our fear is what keeps the old system locked in. The antidote to fear is humanizing each other, being willing to hear the common fear under the rhetoric. If we can do that, we can more gracefully let go of the historical relic of an old system currently in place and move on. Do you know anyone who really feels like the current political system is meeting their needs?

Part of the definition of an ecovillage[40] developed by Robert Gilman of the Context Institute is that it must be human scale, and this guideline seems to me to have a lot of value for any society developing itself deliberately. At the time our founding fathers created this system, it was human scale (at least it was to a scale that could account for the needs of those considered human at the time; remember our original documents were hashed out in a room with about 50 people involved... and the result was considered a "country"!) and it was for a while cutting edge, functional stuff.

One of the results of population growth is an increasing need for flexibility in regularly recreating our systems in order to keep them "human scale" for any given location, region, country, etc. Like Amish communities who grow to a certain size and then split into two communities, we need to be willing to revision and rework ourselves on a regular basis if we want our governance to remain

---

[40] Gilman's definition says that a sustainable community or ecovillage is "human-scaled, full-featured, harmlessly integrates human activities into the natural world, supports healthy human development, with multiple centers of initiative, and can be successfully continued into the indefinite future." There are ecovillages all over the world—some, like Auroville in India, are over 30 years old. They are essentially groups of people who are willing to have their daily lives be part of the experiment

humanistic. And we must do this even if that may mean letting go of the label "American" as anything other than a cultural or social designation indicating people who have lived through this culture's lenses.

Our fear of each other, and fear of not getting our needs met has resulted in an inability to really address the major political themes of our time in a reasonable and creative way. We can't have reasonable, creative conversations about what political system we want because we are trying to talk through and around our own fears, and trying to interpret the words of others through that same fear. The result is that our system seems to have built right into it a bunch of fear. We can't have reasonable, creative conversations about pollution and resource use for the same reason. The system itself gets blamed because it is easier to blame a system than it is to take responsibility for our own fears, and for reaching beyond them.

And it is a vicious cycle. We fear others and it is hard to look at that as something we could handle with some personal responsibility, so we put all our attention on the system, and that brings up even more fear because it is so big and none of us are really happy with it, so we blame it some more, and people who have different complaints about the system become yet another target for our fear ("I mean, I can't possibly trust HIM to revision a system with me!") and then we are really lost in the muck of it all, because we are now multiple steps removed from the original fear.

---

of figuring out just what the heck living sustainably in the modern world means. My "ecohood" in Albuquerque, called Zialua Ecovillage or ZEV, is one such project.

The key to get out of this cycle isn't more analyses. It is simply this: personal responsibility and compassion. Anything else is avoiding the root cause. Stop being afraid of your neighbors, and other ethnic groups, and the "axis of evil" and all the other ways we use neat phrasing to justify and encourage fear. This increase in fear and decrease of trust is the biggest long-term tragedy of 9-11. And it was thoroughly preventable had we been willing to step up to the plate in that moment, admit that this act had scared the hell out of us — a nation who had become accustomed to feeling safe at home. Instead, we retreated from it and attacked back. We essentially just dug the hole deeper, when the answer lies in letting go of those fears. Find within yourself some real compassion.

Everything else is just a distraction.

We have to trust our own intentions, and this can be challenging since we have all done things in our lives that are less than ideal. (Often, we don't trust others because we know how awful people can be to each other — and we know this because we have done it ourselves!) To be able to truly trust our own intentions, we need to have examined them with enough honesty that we have a foundation to build that confidence upon, and to be willing to clean it up when we see ourselves operating from something less than love or Service.

I won't tell you that this challenge goes away, or that new layers don't crop up. But I can tell you that it is worth it, that it gets easier as we build some confidence in our ability to do so. And also that if we truly want the more positive world we can all envision, that this is what is needed. Harry Palmer has said that discouragement is

121

the only thing we really ever have to handle when we are moving toward living our lives in Service, and after a few years of that journey under my belt, it seems to be as accurate an observation as any.

Anything that reduces your ability to be fully responsible for your own life should be set aside. Blaming it (or him or her, if you've got it projected onto another person in your life) just sucks energy away from doing the real work it takes to shift your own life. Vision the systems that work for you, on the small scale of your own life — work the bugs out at the very human scale of your own being, or your own household[41], and you may very well have something real to offer the conversation when it comes to revisioning cultural systems to replace the historical relics we are now all operating with.

So, you say you want a revolution?

Political changes — elections, regime changes, etc. — will only truly matter in the big picture if the people comingintopower have learned to do things fundamentally differently than the old ways of interacting. Base a system on competition, and the people willing to play competitive games will play, and win. I have an old friend who

---

[41] One incredibly useful and fun tool for getting a handle on how sustainable your household is the Ecological Footprint calculator I mentioned earlier. The idea of an Ecological Footprint came out of Mathis and Wackernagel's work. It essentially measures (in acres or hectares) how much of the earth you are personally responsible for utilizing to live the way you live. Several are available to do right on the internet.

used to talk a lot about political revolution, and I remember one particularly intense conversation, during which I said to him, "Yeah, but then what?"

I just didn't see that we—even he and I and our friends who saw ourselves as being so different from the mainstream—had *skills* that were all that different to be able to do something new after the revolution. We'd be new faces, that's all. Our consciousness was not yet different enough for us to be able to truly act differently if we had the power and pressure involved in the job of running a country.

Cultivate people with true ability to come to consensus, be self-responsible and resolve conflicts peacefully, and then you will have a pool of potential leaders who could do things differently in the world. We are not quite there yet—we have not quite yet amassed a critical number of people with these skills, but the work that is being done in personal growth, integrity, mediation and conflict resolution, is training some of the most potent new leadership[42]. It is the success of these movements and others like it that will determine the rate of easy, non-violent, real transformation that we are able to manifest culturally. We are not quite there yet, but it feels close to me. These are the places in which I invest my hope and my own energy, precisely because of this potential.

Being alive at a particular historical juncture generally means

---

[42] One of the reasons I am so dedicated to the Intentional Communities movement is that I see this as one place where all of this type of work is being done very deliberately. In addition to these skills areas, there is also a lot of progress being made on how to live sustainably, how to have gender equity in work, etc. Many

having incarnated with a bunch of other beings that are working on similar stuff. It's like the teachers who have taught enough to be able to say, "If you have a question, ask it, because there are probably other people in the room with the same question." In this case, it is "If you have an issue (be it personal or technical) handle it and share that work with others, because there are probably other people in this life with the same issue."

Our lives are a microcosm of our circle of friends... and of the community in which we live... and the state or province in which we reside... and the country we occupy... and the world around us. Personal transformation—not the self-important wallow-in-analysis or personal misery routine nor the find-a-slicker-way-to-blame-others routine, but real transformational change—is never wasted effort because it IS a contribution to the energy and consciousness of the whole. It is also a small, low-risk testing ground for what works that can ultimately be a model for all those other expanding ripples of life. These ripples are powerful enough to spread out to our community, state, nation and world.

---

communities are like holistic social laboratories with a bunch of willing participants, and that is exciting to me.

Chapter 9: Games Activists Play: Six Traps of Self Importance

"Do my words and actions add to the collective honesty in the world, or the collective dishonesty? Would I like to live in a world where everyone is as honest as I am?"

--From *Living Deliberately*, by Harry Palmer

There are healthy, life-affirming games, like the ones I talked about in the chapter 1, with the metaphor of earth as a playground. Then there are games that are unhealthy and socially damaging. These are the kinds of games evoked by phrases like "playing games with me" and "head games."

This chapter is about the latter type of games. They are the nuts and bolts of what activists do that really doesn't work. Here's a short list of things that undermine the effectiveness of any movement—things I have labeled "Self Importance Traps" because they put our ideas or egos ahead of the good of the movements we love. I have personally done all of these, and so have most of my closest friends involved in this work. They are, in fact, as common as weeds.

Trap #1: My chosen focus is THE issue.

Claiming that our pet issue or pet project is what it is all about is essentially a desecration of others' work. It is a self-importance that abandons teammates, makes less of them, and undermines coalition building. It is bad news for any cooperative endeavor to believe that you have the answer, or even the most important piece of the answer (or even, for that matter, the focus on the most important problem!)

I got into a late-night conversation one night with one of my housemates that started with him relaying a pretty interesting piece from a friend of his who works on cars. This friend was pointing out that any time we burn any kind of fuel, be it gas, diesel or biodiesel, we are consuming not just the fuel, but oxygen in the process. I had never really thought about that, and the possible implications of millions of cars on the road, so that was an interesting thing to contemplate for me. While I had no idea how the science of this would actually shake out, it brought an interesting other factor into the discussion, and as his friend had rightly pointed out, no one is talking about this particular piece of the equation.

The unfortunate thing, though, was that for some reason, this guy felt it necessary to take the conversation on a quick trip into trap #1. He had gone on to say that the political ramifications of a war motivated by protecting our easy access to oil, and the significant pollution problems were "less important" than his observation about oxygen consumption. "Biodiesel is no better than gas" was the final statement, which struck me as being just as shortsighted as what he was addressing in the first place.

To add a piece to the dialogue about fuel was great. But to suddenly make it the only important thing is just self-importance (essentially saying: "My idea is far more important than everyone else's ideas combined") and will ultimately get in the way of people being able to hear the nugget of insight he has to offer. And that's why it's a trap. The need to make our piece overwhelmingly important and diminish the value of other perspectives is a killer to productive, creative dialogue.

Trap #2: Because the improvement I can make now is only a partial solution, and not the end game, I stop myself from acting on my next step.

Growth is always a process. Change, other than catastrophic change, is always a gradual thing. One of the primary failures of the modern environmental movement is encouraging people to believe that if we aren't "sustainable" we are not doing enough. While you could certainly argue that on some level this is true (with some melodramatic perspective that it is only creating a slower slide down into doom) it is a deeply disempowering belief.

Imagine that the progression toward a sustainable lifestyle could be measured on a scale from 0-10. At the beginning, where "0" would be, you have someone who currently doesn't know much or particularly care. Over at "10" you have someone (a mythical someone, probably) who is living a completely sustainable life. In between is where most of us live, and I'd venture a guess that most of us are slowly progressing up the line, becoming more aware, gradually making decisions to be more in alignment with our own are for the planet.

If you are at step #3 in a ten-step process, take step #4! You aren't getting any closer to ten by hanging out at #3 judging yourself. Because many of us have a bit of a perfectionist streak, we will often stunt our own growth because our theory of where we need to get to is so far beyond the step that is right in front of us. (Can you hear the excessive dramatics in that?) It's the equivalent of saying, because I am not perfect, I'm not going to let myself be better. Perfectionism is just self-importance packaged in polite terminology. It is not the same thing as striving to improve or applying yourself to a problem.

It behooves us as educators (and parents, and activists, and simple beings who care) to become better at being gentle yet firm with ourselves in our movement forward, and to have the compassionate perspective that this is a process. This process is one that we can facilitate or hinder with our attitudes.

Have you ever had a sudden revelation about something, and

then tried to change your life radically to fit your revelation? Many of us go through this on occasion. We get an insight into how it could be different, and suddenly we see ourselves at step 7 on our 0-10 scale, we can see ourselves there—just *taste* it. We implement sweeping changes in one fell swoop, and then hold our breath while we try to hold it together.

For most of us, the changes we make in these lightening bolt moments are temporary. It's too much too soon, and while you may be inspired, you haven't yet integrated this new way of being. Slowly the old habits take over again. The net gain from this type of radical overhaul attempt is usually pretty minimal, and may even result in backsliding as you have created evidence for yourself that being more sustainable has to be hard.

Sustainability is both about the content of our lives (what we are actually doing and how that impacts the world) as well as the process. Sustainable changes are the ones you can make that are a stretch but not a stress. This is part of self-care, and when you care for yourself, you are in a better position to know how to care for the planet.

This dynamic of getting stuck because we can't do "enough" is an ego trap because it puts your intellectual ideal for yourself ahead of making any real progress. It is simply self-indulgence.

Trap #3: If others aren't making the same decisions I am, they must not care.

I fall into this one easily. I just don't get how anyone who can afford a new car would buy anything other than a hybrid or a diesel they can run on biodiesel. I just don't get it, and the judgment is part and parcel of the bewilderment. The reality is that people have lots of factors that go into their decisions, and someone who is buying a car I judge to be morally repugnant might very well be way ahead of me in some other department—or perhaps even have a clearer or more enlightened perspective than mine on the topic of eco-friendly vehicles.

Diet is another one that can bring this up for people quite easily—i.e. "If they cared, they wouldn't eat meat." Any successful strategy for social change must take into account, develop and truly honor peoples' free will (as damned frustrating as that can admittedly be at times.) It may be slower, and we may not get what we think we want in all situations, but by honoring peoples' rights to make decisions for themselves, we build their confidence that we are safe to explore with. When we think we know the right answer, we indoctrinate, in doing so we weaken people's capacities to think for themselves.

The reality is that no one is in exactly the same place that we are. I may be ready to leap into an ecovillage and radically alter my resource consumption. But I was raised by an ecologist and have spent years living in communal living situations. I'm not ready to ride my bike everywhere, where someone more athletic than I am might just hop right in to that and only use a car once a week. I cook, and have built up some real confidence in being able to produce really yummy food without meat in it. Someone who has rarely cooked for themselves, or hasn't had much experience with vegetarian food tasting good is probably going to have some transition time if they decide to go to a vegetarian diet. I have never worked in corporate America, so having a loose, creative home-based work scene never involved giving up what we think of as "financial security."

I can let the fact that other people's lives look different become a source of judgment and discouragement, or I can let myself be truly interested in the person, understand where they are coming from, and find out what I can do to support them in their next step. If I just look at them and say, "Drives SUV" and write them off, there is nothing human and honoring in my response. So, tempting as it may be, I make an effort to not go into Trap #3, and stay in appreciation of others as the companions they are on the journey.

Trap #4: I use activism work to build my own ego.

It feels good to be good at something, to have knowledge, to make an impact. When these things play out in a way that is genuinely about being in Service to others, they make a strong, positive impact, and we are willing to really hear feedback from others in those moments that we show up as less than in Service. (After all, if you don't give the ego a big playing field, then it is much less likely to assert itself at inconvenient moments.)

131

When activism work is essentially used as a personal gratification tool, then the results of your work (no matter how copious) will lack clarity and real contributory force in the world. When you have an agenda running other than the one you say you have, you undermine the trust of those around you by acting in a misaligned fashion at those moments when your underlying agenda isn't being met.

For instance, you may agree to be part of planning a conference. Your stated agenda is that you are part of a planning group with the purpose of creating a great weekend event to educate local citizens about water conservation. But maybe you also have a second agenda—to get your name into the papers. Suddenly, instead of having all your attention on what the conference needs, you are silently looking for opportunities to get interviewed; you are less present for the group, and may create tension with your teammates if one of them is the one to get the press. When you are in this mode, it is not just about contributing; it's also about stroking your own ego. And this is a trap.

Trap #5: I'm entitled to _____.

I spent years living with and operating through a sense of entitlement, combined with desperation. Entitlement is another form of ego trip—it is like believing on some level that you are royalty, and others are there to take care of your needs, and do your bidding.

132

My life has begun to open up since I have been shifting from entitlement into asking for support and to put my skills and labor to work in Service to others. The difference is this: entitlement says (internally or out loud) "I am doing good things, so you should _____ (fill in the blank)." Service is quietly committing to your life work, and inviting those with a sincere alignment to join in a project, with no expectation other than that the best in them will join the best in you when it is truly aligned for them to do so. There is no room for reverence within entitlement-based ego-tripping. Reverence comes from putting ourselves into action, in Service. It does not come from expecting that the world is there for you.

Having a sense of entitlement isn't something reserved for men or white people or the upper classes, or whatever other group might be the focus of "privilege" in the various social activism circles. It is a basic competition of animal consciousness, and until we achieve the state of being truly in Service to others as a primary motivation for our lives, this game will occupy at least some of our attention. If we don't feel entitled because we have power of some sort, we feel entitled to be struggling against others to get some.

But all of this is just a game to not take full responsibility for our lives. If I am operating from trying to get something from others, then I am not accepting the full responsibility for meeting my own needs. Instead of just aligned activist energies, people around me have to expend energy to meet some need or desire of mine in order to be able to work with me.

The more productive game is Service to others, and through

133

Service, our needs are met with little effort. So long as we are not *pretending* to be in Service, it is actually a way to get our needs met. People want to support the good work of other people who are showing up.

This same combination of entitlement and desperation is operating in environmental activism. We struggle against the American assumption that we are entitled to drive our cars everywhere, buy cheap goods (with the environmental damage that helps to make them "cheap" occurring in other places) and a thousand other small entitlements that are well documented elsewhere. I won't dwell on the details, because my point is not American bashing.

My point is that this entitlement, so clear outside of us, has a parallel vibe among activists. This entitlement goes something like this: "I'm a good person, doing good work, caring about the earth, and therefore, I should be listened to, and if you aren't listening to me, I will _____." This blank can be filled in with all sorts of things that are less than loving and productive. My own personal version is usually some sort of emotional withdrawal from my teammates (coupled with resentment). Some people go into blame or attack.

It is an equal arrogance to assume we ought to control the dialogue because of a righteous philosophy or good works. We all have our favorite reason why we ought to be honored, taken care of, listened to (in short, why we ought to have some social power). But it's just our pet reasoning. It is no more real or ultimately true than

134

anyone else's pet reasoning. Unfortunately, our activist groups sometimes come together with some (or even most) of us running an entitlement game. The result is that the group becomes a competitive ground for egos vying for attention, rather than a cooperative group aligning around a goal.

Our political system, with its every-four-years struggle for the social power of being the President of the most powerful country in the world is a larger-than-life example of the entitlement game!

No one is entitled to a body, or a place on the earth; no one is entitled to be fed, clothed, and housed. We can set these things as basic goals for everyone to have these things, but not because of entitlement. Rather, these basic "human rights" ought to be available, because we *can* provide them to everyone if we choose to, and they are ethical things to have equally distributed.

We are able to tap into the resources of the universe when we hold them as sacred, and recognize that we are here to be of Service to that world and the other occupants that reside here. Even if someone has riches, entitlement can leave them feeling that they don't have enough. It is a state of mind, an inability to create with grace and ease that I am addressing here. To whatever degree I am not using my unique abilities in Service to others, that is the degree to which I will struggle.

Instead of entitlement, a new belief might be: My needs are met when I show up.

Trap #6: I act from desperation and fear, protecting myself.

When we put our attention on something as large as a planet, and the size of some of the problems we have collectively created on it, it is very easy to find ourselves operating out of fear, and its ego-driven cousin, desperation.

Entitlement and desperation are more closely linked than many people realize. Desperation comes from not trusting ourselves. If entitlement is an expectation that others have some obligation to take care of us, then desperation is actually a natural consequence of this. We learn to expect others to bail us out, and every time that happens, it lowers our confidence level in being able to do it for ourselves. In an ironic and subtle way, winning the entitlement game is actually disempowering to our capacity to create for ourselves, and can feed into us feeling like a victim.

It would be far better for our empowerment if others didn't play the game with us, if, when we are coming from fear and an unwillingness to take care of ourselves, they said no. This is different from those times when we are coming from a sincere effort to be in Service to others, and we create teammates to assist us in doing it easily. It's OK to be paid from work that is in Service, or to have others recognize and appreciate our work. But if the net result of our relationships is an increasing sense of desperation, then we are in trouble.

The planet doesn't benefit from entitlement thinking, nor does it benefit from the energy of desperation. In desperation, instead of having our attention on contributing to something, we gradually turn more and more to protecting ourselves from the (real or perceived) lack of kindness and support in the world.

And any sense of desperation will leak through into our activism work, making us uncomfortable to be around. There is a subtle pressure in the words of a desperate person: Is what you are asking someone to do really all you want them to do? It is as if our energy begs for more than our words are saying. Our words may be asking someone to sign a petition, but our energy is asking, "Save me!" This dynamic creates a lack of trust in our audience; people will frequently respond by trying to get as far away as quickly as possible. It is the opposite of enrolling people in a creative process.

We can all be compassionate with this desperation identity — we have all felt at some point or another like we are in over our heads, and we need to be bailed out. It's a pretty awful feeling to find yourself in. Use your compassion to help your teammates get through this, and ask them to help you with it if they see you doing it. And if you catch yourself in it, take a step back, breathe, and put your attention on being capable.

How much is enough?

My hope is that folks will actually do something with the ideas here — that they aren't just words, but something that you can apply in a practical way in your life. So this begs the question, "How do you know when you've done enough personal work to be able to ethically do activism?" It seems to me that this answer will not look the same for everyone. Some people will feel that they truly need to step back and take a long break from outer world work in favor of a lengthy period of self-inspection. For those who have never really engaged in much personal work, this is probably wise.

But ultimately, I think people come back to action when they feel ready. When you feel like you've learned something new, the best thing is to step back in and test it out in the world again. If you've done some self-reflection, you can get curious about how the world will look different based on this new perspective on yourself. I'd say that when you find yourself *drawn* back in, *and you feel some new humility*, you are probably ready to go another round with the world.

Activism and growth work fold back on each other. I regularly take a week or two to focus on personal work, do what I can during that time, and then come home again to my work. My activism changes, gets stronger and more compassionate and fun, each time. But I also find that each time I come back, I uncover new clues for what's next in my personal work. For me, the two things inch ahead on parallel tracks.

Let me give an example of how these two tracks can inform each other. Several years ago, I resigned from being a co-director of an organization because I had some very difficult dynamics with one of my other co-directors. I felt like my stepping away was both an act of self-care as well as a statement in the world that I was unwilling to support what I was experiencing as disregard for the group good in a fellow leader. I communicated as best I could to the person and my other teammates why I was stepping out, and tried to do my best to tell her in a way that wasn't publicly humiliating and would offer the best chance for her to grow.

Since my previous pattern had been to not address these kinds of dynamics and to just let people get away with behavior that doesn't serve the group, it was a big deal to me to be able to address this calmly and in a way that allowed her to see it as a growth opportunity. Our parting conversation went pretty well and we ended our professional relationship on good terms. The organizational work moved on without me, a few changes happened because of my departure and overall things seemed to be better for all of us. For two years, I felt like this had been the right answer for me in that situation.

But this wasn't the end. As life in a connected community often works, I didn't have the option of burning this particular bridge. My former colleague has continued to be in my life in my ecovillage group, and I found myself recently in a role reversal with her: I was a full member with the power to literally cut her out of the group, and for a while I thought this was what I needed to do. This new group was a lot more important to me than the project we had worked on together previously. It felt like her patterns threatened the health of something very close to my heart, and I started to feel fearful and stressed out.

However, I also noticed that I was really the only one getting triggered by her. Other people saw it and didn't feel like it was great, but no one else was up in the middle of the night torturing themselves about whether or not to request revoking her membership. That was my clue that I still had personal work to do around this person. So, during one of my times out to do personal work, I put her name down on a piece of paper, took a deep breath and contemplated our history together to try to understand how I had gotten to this point with her.

When I looked honestly at our history, it occurred to me that I had never really given her a chance. And when I looked a little closer, I could see that the root of it was a competitive pattern in me: she and I were both working with a woman whom I had a tremendous amount of affection and respect for, and I could see (as I opened myself up to seeing) that I had started off our relationship essentially competing for this third woman's loyalty. I was the new kid on the block with the two of them inviting me into something they had created together, and rather than honor their relationship, I started behaving in an adversarial way. For instance, I was critical of her behavior, especially to our third co-director, and could see how I'd been making subtle efforts to undermine their relationship. Not surprisingly, she responded by behaving badly in turn. I could see that what I perceived as her sabotaging group work was at least in part a *response to my own sabotage of their relationship.*

Where I had previously been focused on her behavior, I was now being willing to own up to the other side of it, and what I discovered is that I had actually started it. She never had a chance. And our entire relationship was built on that skewed foundation. I realized that I was never going to see her actions clearly or know what the right thing to do with her was until I dropped my own competitive lens. It was a painful thing to look at, especially having to accept that I had caused pain to the very person I was seeking love and affection from as she watched her two beloved companions struggle with each other.

The payoff for doing my work, however, was worth it: for the first time, I was able to understand what had been baffling to me: the old question, "Why would someone behave like that?" suddenly had a logical answer, and the relief I felt was palpable. Best of all, because it was an answer that I had a role in, I could contribute to changing it.

This is what I've taken away from the story. At the time I got into this organization, what I was working with as my own growth edge was power dynamics and being willing to speak. This was a very important step for me, and being able to do my personal work and then act on it out there in the world was critical to my growth and to raising the bar on my own integrity as an activist. Two years later, I was working on other issues — primarily related to my own leadership and how I enroll or discourage teammates — and from this perspective, I could see new pieces of the puzzle.

I wouldn't have seen those pieces if I wasn't willing to continue engaging in activism work. This is the cycle for me: activism gives me clues about my personal work, my personal work strengthens my activism, which gives me clues as to the next steps on my personal work, etc. It is more spiral than linear line.

So, was my earlier response of stepping out of our joint

141

projects wrong? Did my later work somehow invalidate my earlier work? I think the answer is no. I think that in an evolutionary process, where one is sincerely engaged and doing the best we can with the information and level of willingness to look at ourselves that we have at the time, we act as best we can, trust that this will be better than it would have been without any self-examination, and be willing to re-examine things later if need be.

At the time that I stepped out, stepping out *was* a healthier pattern than what I had been doing (which was some version of submission). Now that I can see a still healthier way to be with her, I am obligated to act on that one. I am certain, however, that I wouldn't have gotten where I am now had I not passed through that earlier phase with her.

The trick is learning to be OK with never being done. Truth changes as we progress. Doing better is doing our best, and continuing to push ourselves to do better is the path of real growth. Harry Palmer says, "The prize of experience is perspective: everything else is just information."[43] The more we experience with our eyes open, the more perspective we are going to gain, and truth looks different from different or bigger perspectives. What felt complete from one perspective may be reopened with a new perspective: a larger "you" is available to contemplate the larger meaning of your actions. You have to act with faith that this will happen—you can't rush a larger being into existence, you have to be willing to go through the process to get there. And in the meantime, the world needs us to keep acting on its behalf.

Looked at from this angle, there is not some set moment when you are 100% "ready" to be an ethical activist. Rather, it is the willingness to be in the *process* of becoming more ethical that is important. Knowing that it is a process of always getting better, you have to be willing to not give up when you realize in hindsight that you weren't perfect. If you are ready to commit to having your life include self-reflection and growth, then you have taken the first step to becoming a more ethical activist, and that is all anyone can ask. You act from that place, reflect on what happened, make changes and then act again.

"Ready" is a slippery concept: "Am I ready?" is a great question with lousy prospects for coming up with a definitive answer. You should ask it anyway! The positive side is that it can encourage you to ask yourself needed questions and be humble in light of your ongoing growth. The negative is that it can be a self-defeating concept that stifles your willingness to act in the world. There is no sure answer, and this mystery and risk is part of the territory of a self-reflective life.

Here's a metaphor for the visually inclined: Think of your growth with any given situation as a series of pictures taken of the same scene, each one from a few feet further back. Every step on our growth path can be seen as being an advancement to the next picture in the series — we see more each time, and things look different as you

---

[43] *Love Precious Humanity*, Harry Palmer, 1999.

are able to include more in your picture of what happened. In the first frame, you might just be able to see yourself feeling isolated, hurt and angry: take that picture and focus on that first. Really allow yourself to own this experience and be compassionate with yourself for the tough place you were in. In the next, you may be able to also see the shocked look on the face of the person you were so angry with: take another picture and contemplate that person's feelings and role, and how your anger may have impacted them. In the third, you may actually be able to see all of the supportive companions that were in the room with you: hmm... maybe you weren't so alone after all? And how was it for those folks? Was anyone trying to reach out to you? Eventually, you'll be able to see that outside of the room, the world was serene and sunny: now there's perspective! It all happened in a small bubble.

The blessing of doing our work is being able to focus on that serenity, and let some of the old charge dissolve. Take the gift of the sunny world outside and let it heal you.

This is the value of gaining broader perspective; just like I could only see my colleague's action in that earliest snapshot I took, but eventually, I was able to see all of the relationships interwoven, and my own role in the thing. Eventually, you grow enough that the close-up "you" in that first picture is hardly recognizable as the "you" that is now viewing it. Using the approach helps you shake loose your fixed ideas of what any given scenario was or means. Your experience was your experience from where you were sitting... and there was also a lot more going on.

144

One of the tougher challenges implied in this type of work is that we need to be vulnerable enough to be able to admit to our changing truth as we become more self-honest. Going back to my colleague and admitting that my perspective on her had changed, that I now believe I had treated her unfairly and that I am feeling more open to working with her took a particular kind of courage: not only did I have to admit that I was wrong to her, but I also have to backtrack and admit to a whole group of people that my prior, firmly held analysis was flawed. I have multiple relationships to reorient, and all of them have a public aspect.

The willingness to endure public embarrassment is part of the life of a self-aware activist. The good news is that people generally respond well to the vulnerability. People will trust you more if they see you can change.

Chapter 10: Right Livelihood, Wrong Volunteerism

"[Right Livelihood is] living in a totally authentic way, with no separation between work life and personal life."

--Peter LeBrun, *On the Path to Right Livelihood*

Sometimes I feel like volunteerism is a double-edged sword. On the one hand, volunteering gives us a creative outlet for Service. On the other hand, it can distract us from our pursuit of right livelihood.

Geoph Kozeny traces right livelihood all the way back to Buddha[44]. He says, "Originally, it meant doing honest work and harming neither another person nor any living thing." He offers a modernized definition: "It's the art of clarifying what it is you are passionate about, then finding a way to make your living in pursuit of

---

[44] Geoph wrote about right livelihood in the editorial of the fall 2003 *Communities* magazine (#119) a fine resource for anyone interested in intentional community.

that passion... No longer is a teacher or higher authority required to determine what qualifies; the evaluation process has become personalized to the extent that each individual decides for himself/herself what's worthy and what's not."

Certainly, one can volunteer in an area he or she is passionate about, so on the surface it seems to be a compatible thing, and often it is. There's a downside, though. Volunteerism can serve a similar role in the work world that recycling sometimes plays in the world of eco-activism. How many times have you heard someone say, "Oh yeah, I care about the environment, I recycle!" This is a case of one good act being used as a smokescreen to mask an otherwise unconscious life. In the overall arena of environmental responsibility, there are literally hundreds of acts one could undertake. By focusing on one of these acts as complete evidence of care, we take a very narrow view. Put another way, it isn't evidence of a *lifestyle* of care so much as a selective tuning into *one act* of care.

We all want to look good. In pursuit of this, we often publicly cultivate certain acts, certain places in our lives where we are living our values (or, sometimes, living the values we think others want us to live) and then privately let ourselves off the hook from looking at all the other areas.

Now, I hesitate to go too far with this, because this can lead to the same thinking that some people use to really beat up on others in their lives, or on themselves—the "you aren't doing enough" approach. This is NOT where I want this to go. Nor do I wish to give the impression that I think volunteerism (or recycling, for that matter)

148

is a bad thing.

I want this to head somewhere much more subtle, and that is looking at our *own* values, and our *own* acts with the intention to explore which ones are coming from real alignment and which ones are coming from an attempt to draw people's attention away from those parts of our lives that WE, ourselves, feel could be better. The ego is a powerful thing. We want to look good; we want to be right. But the incredible energy it takes to be right and look good is energy that the world needs right now to be redirected into real, aligned Service.

My experience has been that when we stop defending our lack of alignment, and creating schemes to draw people's attention away from it, all that energy going into defenses and scheming becomes available to us to take the daily steps of being more aligned. It takes energy to defend ourselves (think of how exhausting it can be to argue with your mate). *This is especially true if the defense is partly designed to defend our actions against our own internal wisdom.*

So back for a moment to volunteerism. How many of us stay in jobs that occupy a huge percentage of our energy, and then work at doing the right thing (for ourselves, or our own creative dreams, or the planet) in our "off hours"? But try this on: "I am in part-time Service to others to try to make up for my full-time destruction of my personal vision for how I want the world and my life to be." Ouch! Suddenly all the ancient religious doctrine about doing atonement for "sin" has a modern application...[45]

There is a solution, a long-term one that requires you becoming more committed to your own highest vision for your life and the planet, and that is this: *Cultivate a life that doesn't need to be atoned for.*

One of the arguments that keep us locked into our destructive work choices is that there aren't enough "cool" jobs out there for everyone. And in the current economic and social systems, that may be true. We (and I'm going to say we here, because there are many, many people out there advocating for similar things) are suggesting something that is about a major cultural shift in values. If you didn't want life in general to look different, though, I don't think you would have picked this book up.

Let me address this question of "not enough cool stuff" in a couple of ways. First, realize that many, many lines of work can either be destructive or creative, depending on *how* we do them. There is a positive role for reform within many companies and many industries, and there isn't a right answer as to whether or not you give something up and switch work. Look with open eyes at your company, your job and your products or services with the question, "Is how and what I am doing with my time truly in Service to the world?" This may reveal ways that it could be changed to be in

---

[45] I would bet that if there is any truth in what I am saying here for you, that last paragraph hurt. I'm blessed in my life with having people who help me find the ouches and then sit with me while I work through them so I'm not trapped in those contradictions and not stuck in living only part way up to my own life. My hope is that you have people who do the same for you.

Service, or those places in your life where there is room for improvement.

You may also be able to keep doing your work, but change *what you are doing it on behalf of.* In other words, work for one company may be destructive, while doing the same basic work for another could have a positive impact. This may or may not involve a pay cut (because our culture is in transition, and doesn't yet place full market value on Service to others) but then again it may not (because we ARE part way into that transition). If it does, just recognize that money is energy, but it is only one kind of energy, and you will have far more of those other types of energy from doing good work than you currently have from a bigger paycheck. The people I know who are most fully living in Service to others would put the energizer bunny to shame, and they live lives that, contrary to popular belief, do not suffer from lack on the material plane.

Now the second answer I have to the "not enough cool jobs" issue is that this is, in and of itself, something that we need to address as a culture. What the majority of us do for a living is reflective of what we, as a culture, value. We often feel the lack of opportunities for real human connection, for really nurturing health care and food, for art and opportunities for creative expression and personal growth, and other interesting, nurturing resources. Meanwhile, we are flooded with access to stuff and readily available jobs to maintain our stuff.

Many of us who are making it doing "alternative" work are doing so by piecing together a number of strands of these things. For instance, at the time that I started working on this book, I was also delivering the Avatar course, teaching grant writing and sustainability classes, doing some organic natural foods catering, working part-time as the Program Director for a nonprofit, and managing the logistics of my community — not primarily because I had to do all these things, but because diversity is fun. And not all of these activities are done just for money; I also do some bartering and exchange.

We don't have the apparent security of a 9-5 job with health insurance and paid vacations. We have, instead, a life of creative living, real connections and the extra energy that comes from knowing we are doing what our hearts have called us to do. We also have tremendous flexibility, and we don't have to be afraid that if one thing we are doing goes out of vogue, we'll be left without options, or that our skills won't be applicable to the changing job market, because we have so many skills we are actively cultivating. And while I don't have any hard evidence for this, it sure seems like we are on the whole much healthier people, reducing our reliance on health insurance.

We are also typically engaged in work that has a lasting value outside of fads. It is the difference between building homes that last for 50 years versus building homes that last for 500. There have been healers and builders for many, many thousands of years, and artists and musicians, and spiritual counselors and ministers, and growers and preparers of food. These are examples of timeless, cross-cultural work of real value, meeting timeless needs.

And there are, of course, better and worse ways to do any of these things. Take, for instance, the difference between using a law degree to do mediation work that fosters real understanding versus being a cutthroat, divisive legal "counsel."

I was part of a group a few years ago that was looking at the question of what ethical business practices were and how we could tell if we were engaged in them or not. One of the criteria we came up with was that an ethical business is one that recognizes and meets a real human need; an unethical business is one that creates a need or desire to be addressed and puts itself in the position of filling that (newly created) "need." Perhaps the best question under all of this is asking, "Whose benefit is this company or product being created for?" and if the answer is the company itself, then it is not likely to be something that is in Service to others.

Doing business for the sake of doing business is rarely of benefit to the planet, because that simply isn't the intention behind it. By the same token, governmental programs that encourage a rise in the Gross National Product for its own sake rarely ripple out in a real positive increase in our quality of life. A government program that gave grants for the pursuit of right livelihood—or teaching children how to recognize what is truly right for them—would be a quite different animal! And one, perhaps, of enlightened government.

In the course of looking at creating a positive work culture, one of the other traits that we seem to have in common among those who have made the leap into Service to others as a primary motivator is that we also *cultivate each other*. I use money to support people who are doing other work of real value. I shop at the food coop or other companies that have as a primary goal planetary health; I get massages from friends who are truly committed to healing; I buy art, or go to workshops, or send my son to a great program, or send money to organizations that are cultivating good works in the world. Or I loan money to someone trying to get a new business off the ground or going to a meaningful personal growth course, or I put it into installing a better grey water recycling system at our house.

In other words, money IS energy, and we can direct it toward those places and with those people who are most aligned with Service to the planet. If I wouldn't talk up a company that is actively acting against my values and the planet's health, why would I put money into it? The simple direction of money toward aligned businesses is part of how we support a cultural transition toward right livelihood.

My hope is that, like "alternative" music stations of a decade ago, "alternative" work will shortly become the "top 40". Of course, being willing to commit to right livelihood requires a big vision. And that is where we are headed next.

Chapter 11: Embodying Enlightened Activism: Ananda's Story

Defining a new way of being is like assembling a puzzle—but without the benefit of the picture on the box.

I'm spinning my way through pieces, falling between the intellect and my felt sense of what I want to say. It has something to do with forgiveness, something to do with embodiment and incarnation, something to do with the relationship between our spiritual development and how we express it in the world.

Wander with me for a while...

I am pregnant. My usual mental sharpness is dulled in the natural sea of hormones that makes it possible for a woman to cocoon herself in the world of making a baby and prioritize it above all else for a time. It is a species-level survival tactic, and while I am grateful for it, it is damned

frustrating for an Aquarian. Feels like your closest friend has abandoned you
when the mind loses its sharpness. (Dec. 2004)

When I began this project, I made a commitment to myself to take whatever was happening in my life and use it as reflective material for the book. We can't separate our lives from our activism. We are activists because we see things in the world that affect real people's real lives, and we are unwilling to sit by and let things go unaddressed and unacknowledged. We see business practices that have separated life from business; we see political decisions that feel disconnected from the people they affect most strongly. These separations and disconnects violate our sense of ethics.

So I know after years of working with this approach that there can be no separation between the major parts of my life. If I am writing a book all about the earth and honoring incarnation as a gift, and I get unexpectedly pregnant in the midst of it, I have to ask myself what the relationship is between these things. It is not simply that I have created something new that is compromising my mental acuity (though self-sabotage is certainly one of the tapes I run in my own mental landscape). There is also something about keeping my activism real at the level of birth and death and life itself; staying real within the fog that producing life brings on.

It is a reminder that we do this work because we are all actively engaged in life, and that we cannot stop paying attention to the world around us, no matter how compelling and positive the sphere of our daily lives may be, no matter how much there are Big

Things (or Busy Things) happening for us that draw the bulk of our attention to our smaller worlds of self and family.

How do we do even the most mundane of activities with our values firmly in place? How do we do life itself with the importance of honoring that life built right into the daily routine? How do we hold things as sacred that are the very fabric of everyday life, those things that most people treat as mundane? So many of us walk around dull and uninspired, and I am coming to believe that this is precisely because we treat our lives as mundane, and therefore treat life itself as dispensable and unworthy of honoring.

Come May, I will, for the second time in my life, spend a day standing at the doorway between life and death and from my willingness to stand there, a new life will come into the world. Without treating this as an important (monumental even) moment and therefore treating the build-up to it as important, I will be desecrating something that, far from being a flash in the pan, is actually the essence of life itself. (Jan. 2005)

We are sacred beings playing with the reality of having a human form. Our collective playground is earth. Our purposes may vary depending on our own karma and choices we make, but I guarantee that for all of us there is something bigger than paying the bills and watching TV.

So, somehow, being an activist is about our mundane existence, as well as our inspiration. But that's not the whole answer. There are other pieces, too, and one piece that I can wrap my head around right now is forgiveness. Harry Palmer says, "You have done and can do no wrong I do not share." And more than any other line in Harry's work, I feel this one in my bones.

From one perspective, there is nothing to forgive. And yet, forgiveness is a challenge that appears so regularly on the horizon of human landscape, it can hardly be ignored when we talked about growth and evolution.

It is a loaded term for many of us. We think it is about saying what someone did is OK, letting it slide, that forgiveness means not being properly acknowledged for some wrong done to us, for our very real hurt. This is not the version of forgiveness I am talking about. It is not a soft, avoidance-based new age ideal; forgiveness is a deeply pragmatic act, and a damned difficult skill to master.

When we don't forgive, we don't move on. This is what it does to us. We also can easily find ourselves meeting a wrong with a new wrong—punishing someone for years for something they did to us that we consider unforgivable. If we want to change and grow then we must be willing to forgive.

I discovered this winter that I had been holding on to resentment against my brother for having "abandoned" me my senior year in high school. Mark is a year older than me, and he did what most of us do when they graduate—he re-established an independent life as quickly as possible and the bulk of his attention went to that new life, two hours away. He hadn't actually done anything wrong, but in my 17-year-old mind, I was left behind and lonely. For twenty years, I felt this abandonment, but it was subtle enough that I didn't even really notice it—I just knew we weren't as close as we used to be, and I wrote it off as the consequence of growing up and living in different states.

One evening over a few beers, my sister-in-law and my husband pinned the two of us down and asked a few pointed questions about why two usually connected and engaged people were so content with our distanced relationship. I fought their feedback in the moment, but on the train on the way home, I started to think about what Laird and Kim had said, and suddenly broke down crying, realizing that I *missed* my big brother--horribly. I realized that the only real barrier to us being closer was my lack of forgiveness for this perceived slight. When I got home, I wrote him a long letter talking about my feelings from back then, my perceptions of us now, and mostly just saying that I was sorry for the role I'd played in our distance. Mark's response was as warm and welcoming as I could have wanted (and it still brings tears to my eyes writing about this). I could have remained resigned to it, but thanks to the willing feedback of people who love us, we are developing a real relationship again.

This is the power of forgiveness.

The first step is simply to acknowledge--and I mean really acknowledge, not just say it to ourselves--that we all screw up. Being human means making mistakes, and sometimes it also means we hurt each other because we feel powerless to do anything else. Sometimes it is completely inadvertent (like my brother just doing his thing, without any real intention to hurt me). Without forgiveness (and by this I mean both internal self-forgiveness and forgiving the person who did something that hurt us) people can stay stuck. We can't afford to stay stuck.

At a time when we have rapidly accelerated our ability to destroy ourselves via technology, forgiveness becomes essential on a larger and larger scale. The bigger the potential impact of our acts, the bigger we have to grow in spirit, and the acts of real apology and acceptance, which lay the groundwork for real forgiveness and learning, take a real stretch of the human spirit.

Imagine for a moment every mistake you have ever made. Feel them pile up on you. Imagine that you had never moved on from them — that your growth stunted at the moment you messed up and you were simply doomed to keep repeating it over and over again. It's like the movie *Groundhog Day*, except you are caught in your worst moment.

Now imagine that on a cultural level. Imagine a United States still actively practicing slavery, still as thoroughly sexually repressive as we were in the 1950's. Maybe we would have dropped more nuclear bombs had we not learned just how awful it was and decided to exercise a bit more discretion; maybe we'd still be using DDT as bug killing juice; maybe we'd still be committing people en masse to institutions for exploring their homosexuality. Imagine the wasteland of life we could have created for ourselves by continuing to act fully as badly as we know we are capable of acting.

This is a picture of life without forgiveness and learning. We repeat our mistakes until they are discharged.

160

Notice those moments of genuine forgiveness you have had in your life. A friend of mine once made a beautiful apology to myself and two others; he invited us over to a pillow-filled room with candles and food and sat us down and confessed that his heart was hurting for something he had done. There were no excuses, and his remorse was genuine. Over the course of his speaking to us, I found myself reconnecting after a painful week of separation. Suddenly the act mattered a lot less than his honesty and vulnerability.

Have you ever had a moment like that, when someone owned up to something? It can shift your whole being, and open the door to things that seem miraculous: maybe you can view something from your childhood, and instead of returning to the perspective of a hurt child, you were suddenly able to have some perspective where you understood, and in that moment forgave. Or maybe you can talk to a lost friend again, or let go of a resentment that has held you back.

It doesn't mean we forget what was done; it just means we are able to move on from it without holding resentment. Forgetting means we are denying the lesson, and that is one thing the world does not need right now. Forgiveness, in fact, allows us to see the lesson clearly, unclouded by hurt. After my friend's confession, I started being able to see how I had played into the situation, and was able to learn something from it that had been clouded previously by our disconnection.

What can you forgive our government for? What can you forgive corporations for? Can you let go of your own small emotional hurts on behalf of opening the door for global transformation? What can you forgive so that you can move on to being able to see *their* actions and *their* perspectives clearly?

The difference between a disagreement and a fight is emotional charge. Honest disagreement as a starting place has the potential to be transformed into the highest expression of living and deciding together — real consensus and alignment. Starting a fight is essentially creating an opportunity to hurt someone else because you need to be right.

Consensus means we listen enough to hear the nugget of truth from everyone, and then get bigger than the apparent contradictions to find something that works for everyone. Alignment goes even beyond that — it is where our deepest felt values are shared and expressed in an effortless way. We are, culturally, still struggling with might makes right, and our highest aspiration is a democracy expressed in the voting system of winners and losers.

We need to set our sights higher, and start the daily work of showing that consensus and alignment are not only possible, but they are more sustainable alternatives to either of the dominant paradigms we currently operate with. Peace can't flourish with either might makes right or majority rule. They are antithetical to people really feeling heard and having their needs met, and on a cultural level, you need both for real peace. The environmental destruction inherent in not having peace will eventually exhaust both the planet and its inhabitants.

Think of the energy it takes to keep an argument with a family member going for years, and how draining that is for you personally.

162

Now multiply that by the number of people involved in a war; no wonder creative, peaceful resolution to some of our more stubborn conflicts in the world are in short measure! When we lack forgiveness, and can't see each other as human beings and lay down our conflicts, there is not a lot of energy left for creativity.

Again, let me return to the major theme of this book. It must begin at home.

We cannot expect people in some foreign land "doing horrible things to each other" to lay down their conflicts if we have not first shown the viability and vibrancy of laying down our own smaller conflicts. It would be hypocritical to do so, and so long as we stand outside and want someone else to do it, we are simply sitting in judgment—judgment that is not only unhelpful, but hopelessly naïve. We don't *know* what it takes to lay down a conflict, if we refuse to do it ourselves. We don't *know* what it takes to really listen to someone we have judged as being in the wrong, if we refuse to do it ourselves. We don't *know* what it takes to transform an enemy into a cooperative ally if we refuse to do it ourselves. And we don't *know* what it takes to truly apologize and be vulnerable enough to ask for forgiveness, if we refuse to do it ourselves.

Until we know in our bones the spiritual strength it takes to do these things, the world will remain locked into war, and the earth will continue to head into a slow death. That's the bad news. The good news is that as more people commit our lives to doing this work, the tide slowly shifts.

You can't have peaceful, lasting conflict resolution without

163

forgiveness. You may have a cease-fire, but it will only be temporary. Consciousness is a neutral thing; it will continue to present to us the opportunity to do our work, be it forgiveness or something else, until we do so, regardless of the consequences on the physical plane.

You can't fake it in the realm of consciousness. It is, in its own way, a place of absolutes. Eventually an unresolved conflict will start up again, seemingly having a life of its own, unless the process of peace is completed. And it will never be complete without forgiveness. It may go underground, and move from guns and bombs into social prejudice, discrimination and "petty" violence, but it won't truly end. This incompletely resolved tension and tendency to re-erupt is the fragile peace that have kept queens, presidents, clan leaders and prime ministers (and not a small number of their advisors) sleepless at night since the dawn of time.

The antidote is forgiveness.

Applying the Lesson

I say that, and it feels right. Now, can I apply it to myself?

In the midst of the first trimester body adjustment, I have just lost two weeks on my timeline for this project, just when I had gotten into a rhythm with it and started feeling like a release date of Earth Day 2005 was doable. That missed deadline is a result of sleeping through a large chunk of my usual productive hours for the past few weeks. This wasn't exactly what I had in mind when I said I'd incorporate whatever was happening in my life into the fabric of the book, but it is what I have created.

"What on God's green earth," I've been asking myself, throwing up my mental hands, "could an unplanned pregnancy have to do with writing a book about human consciousness and the environmental movement?" We embody what we believe; we invite creations into our lives via our consciousness.

Alberto, my partner in this pregnancy, and I already have three kids between the two of us. We had already talked about both being clear that we didn't want more kids. Meanwhile, at the ages of 47 and 34 (and therefore being "old enough to know better") we managed to get ourselves knocked up. Such is biology. Such, too, is our ability to create opportunities for ourselves for the aforementioned act of forgiveness, and for the creative problem solving that can kick in when you don't yield to the temptation to blame and make someone else wrong.

One of my Co-Directors with The Sustain Ability Trust is a beautiful, amazing Brazilian woman named Zaida. She and her husband, Denis, have been talking about adopting a baby for the better part of a year. As soon as I realize that I really am pregnant, my community-builder's wheels start to turn. They are dear friends and part of our extended community. This child even has a rough genetic mix not too different from theirs — Alberto's genes are primarily Mexican-Mestizo, with a smidge of German, and I am a European Heinz 57; Zaida has a mix of mestizo and European blood in her veins, and Denis a mix of French-Canadian European and native blood. It seems like a sign; this child could be theirs.

We slowly make the shift from panic to creativity, though the *vigilance it takes to not blame each other is tiring by itself. We are now having a child for two incredible people whom we really love, and unlike most adoption situations, we plan to have a strong presence in this child's life. And this child is already creating being aligned with her biological mother's legacy of creating community – to start life with four parents planning on having some involvement in your life is a pretty phenomenal way to begin!*

It has been a challenging, time and heart-consuming few weeks for all of us, and a process that has left us all a little in awe of how things sometimes unfold. (Oct. 2004)

But what does all this have to do with writing this book? Sometimes, we create a circumstance in our consciousness, and then in our lives, that looks like a disaster, looks like the last thing you would possibly want to create.

It is at those moments in our lives that we have choices – how will I deal with this? Alberto and I could have blamed each other (men and women do that all the time – they get pregnant and it turns into a big resentment-fest immediately, and you've suddenly alienated your closest ally). We could have immediately gotten an abortion, and tried to "move on" (whatever *that* means) in spite of our own gut-level feeling that it wasn't the best thing for us, and in spite of knowing there was an unmet need in our community that we could fill, that Zaida and Denis wanted a child so much it hurt. An abortion in this case would have essentially meant not being creative enough to step up to the plate and find a solution that was really in Service to everyone. We could have resigned ourselves to raising another child, and taken the attitude that we are at the effect of life, instead of in charge of our own lives. We could have tortured ourselves with the possibilities for weeks, until we just became so deeply frustrated that we made a bad decision out of sheer mental exhaustion.

Or we could have done what we did. We accepted responsibility for having created the situation, looked at the whole big picture of our lives and our community, and took it as a creative opportunity instead of a tragedy. The bonus in taking the route that we took was that Zaida and Denis were also able to be in Service to us as a couple. I believe that it is our Service orientation, plus our ongoing willingness to do consciousness work, that has made it possible for us to do this adoption with joy and integrity. This in spite of warnings from various people (personal and professional) that how we were going about it (everything from my breast feeding to us conceptualizing ourselves as a family, and therefore being the most "open" of adoptions[46]) was a bad idea, and ultimately would somehow damage Ananda.

As activists, we too have to make these types of decisions: complex ones that ask us to dig deep into our values and take risks. Do we accept what shows up in our lives as a manifestation of our

---

[46] Adoptions are generally broken into two classifications: open and closed. Open adoptions are those where the child knows their birth parent(s) with varying degrees of involvement; closed are ones where documents are sealed and there is no intention of having an ongoing relationship between the families. Our adoption agent (who was actually a remarkable woman who took interacting with us as a learning opportunity and did a fabulous job of balancing out traditional wisdom with an

own consciousness, even when it feels big and overwhelming? Do we step up to the plate in that moment with understanding, and a commitment to stay connected to our co-creators? Or do we dissolve into blame and mentally exhaust ourselves with our hopelessness?

What's really practical?

Now, months after writing the previous section, I have had another baby, been the pass-through for another human to get a body. I did this in an already crowded world, and I'm a dedicated environmentalist. Mistakes and forgiveness and creative action are spun together in the flesh of our collective daughter, who was named Ananda Maya. Perhaps, these are the things of flesh itself, and every one of us embodies this same dance.

Can I somehow measure my own decision to have this child adopted by friends against my own emerging definition of enlightened activism? I said earlier that enlightened activism is "the outward thrust into the world of a value I hold for a better world" where that value is one that I have cultivated through my spiritual work, grounded in integrity and compassion. By that definition, does this qualify?

I look at the values I have cultivated. Some of them are: community, taking responsibility for what I create, Service to others. I saw another value as well, one evening during our pregnancy while meeting with my ecovillage group. It is simply this: I care. About myself, and others around me. About the planet. And it seems to me

openness to helping us explore what this was going to look like for us) told us that this was "the *most* open adoption" she'd ever handled.

that Alberto and I chose the most care-filled option we could: for ourselves and Ananda and Zaida and Denis and the children we already had.

This morning, another piece falls into place. I've talked about this adoption to everyone. Literally. Any stranger who noticed that I was pregnant and had more than a minute was a candidate for hearing about the adoption. Friends got more detail—the blow-by-blow of the emotional sea of being a birth-mother, all our hopes, the little shopping trips, the fears passed to us by the adoption agency and our process of working through the doubts, what my body was doing that day. We had some fears initially that we were doing something that would offend people, that it was just too risky, too outside of the box and people would react with judgment.

But what I've found is that we *give* people something with our story. People feel hopeful that we took this risk, giving so literally of ourselves in order to feed the joy of others, and that we are doing this together, as a community. I had strangers moved to tears, and "god bless you's." I sat one night on the ground just a few weeks before Ananda was born with my neighbor, Helen, as we both weeded on our sides of the fence, and we talked about our lives—her with a new grandbaby and her own personal history of pain and joy with her children, and me with this story, and we got to know each other because we were willing to open up with each other.

In those moments, I know this child and her story are a gift to the bigger world, too. We are in a moment of cultural transition with some basic concepts, including what family means. The more of us

169

who are willing to do this revisioning publicly — be it with an adoption like ours, gay marriages, having cooperative and caring relationships with our co-parents after a divorce, etc. — and particularly as we interface with public agencies like the courts, the press or adoption agencies, the more we give courage and hope to each other. So it isn't simply that we have an unusual family — that it is big and clunky and joyful and is only partially about blood — it is also that this chosen family offers something both profound and concrete that lets people dream. *It's about caring enough to risk sharing the story and inspiring hope in others.*

There's that word again: care. At the bottom of it all, there is care.

This for me is the heart of the enlightened activist identity. This soft, open caring, this willingness to be an inspirer of hope, and new possibilities. We can build the other things out from there — the passion and optimism and everything else. But at the core, there is simply, "I care."

Because of Ananda, I understand at a deeper level the importance and the impact and this core of enlightened activism. So, in this way, she has given another gift to the world.

Chapter 12: Context and Community

"Nothing cripples the will like isolation. By the same token, nothing buoys the spirit and fosters hope like the knowledge that others faced equal or greater challenges in the past and continued on to bequeath us a better world. Even in a seemingly losing cause, one person may unknowingly inspire another, and that person yet a third, who could go on to change the world, or at least a small corner of it."

--From the introduction to *The Impossible Will Take a Little While*, edited by Paul Rogat Loeb

oes context matter? In an absolute sense, it really doesn't. Your ethics and responsibility for your own life and impact are yours, and yours alone. But in the practical reality of daily life that we operate in, context can make a tremendous difference in how easy it is for us to keep rolling with our noblest goals, keep showing up as our best and most contributory selves.

And our context can be changed. We can get out of abusive relationships and suddenly the world looks different. We can move to a part of the country that supports our body's health, and have more vibrancy to call on. We can create a new group of friends that are on a wavelength we are striving to embody, and have support for our own changing consciousness. We can live in the city so we can get rid of our cars, or live in the country to be able to grow more of our own food, etc.

Context is changeable, just as consciousness is; at the bottom line, context, too, is a choice.

There are thousands of factors that feed into making the context of one's life the best fit to support our goals and the easy development of our values. And it is not going to be the same for everyone. I'm going to offer a perspective, though, that I think cuts across a lot of lines and gets to something universal, or close to it. *I believe that we all do better when we are held within a supportive, aligned community of people.* This can mean anything from having a positive, supportive family scene, to having a strong circle of friends with aligned values, to living in an intentional community that has come together to specifically support the goals you are most interested in pursuing.

The shifts I am calling for here are not minor, nor necessarily obvious. Having close companions to help you grow and change can be invaluable. Good friends can keep us honest and help us not get pulled into discouragement. My ex-husband is a yoga teacher, and one of his Indian teachers used to say that the biggest challenge for Americans is that we believe we can and have to go it alone. Our independence can be a real strength, but the stubborn disconnect that can creep in along with it can be incredibly debilitating if it stops us from creating (and accepting) support.

For the majority of the time I was working on this book, I lived in a small intentional community of 10 people in Albuquerque NM. Our two neighboring houses functioned as a community, and we were further connected to a number of other co-op houses and community-oriented people in Albuquerque. Although we aren't all still living together, we have community together in the best sense of the word—people who are aware of each other's lives and interests, who show up and are real for each other.

While we shared space, we supported each other in a myriad of ways. We helped each other parent and do our art and work and relationships well. We shared early morning coffee in the kitchen, and late night hummus on the living room floor. We hung out and relaxed together and talked politics and spiritual growth and daily annoyances, and we helped each other find solutions to our challenges that didn't involve stomping on someone else in the process; and when we screwed up and hurt each other, the rest of the group helped us to work through it and get reconnected.

We are part of a global movement toward peaceful conflict resolution, ecologically sound life choices, deeply caring about the fate of planet and people, and becoming more and more personally responsible. To have that embodied in the companions of our daily lives was an incredible boost for all of us.

These are people who inspire me and help me grow, people who don't let me get away with being dishonest or cruel or lazy or hiding; these are the people who help me balance my life, and whom I get to be in Service to in helping them balance theirs. None of them are as active in sustainability issues as I am, but community isn't about being clones of each other; in fact, in many ways healthy community is about supporting each of us finding our unique voice in the world.

I came to the conclusion about 7 or 8 years ago that real, lasting global change is going to happen if many, many fronts are worked on simultaneously, and while it is all work that needs to be done, I can't personally do it all. I no longer seem to have the temperament for edgy activism, nor for academic research; I see the value of work on poverty and disability issues, economic and health-care reform, and a thousand other things, but have never taken a direct interest in working in those arenas explicitly. I dabble in art and music, but leave the deeper exploration of those arenas to others.

My own pieces seem to be more about personal consciousness, ecological sustainability, community building, and healing the split between the practical and the beautiful. These are the pieces I am easily, joyfully passionate about. They are no more important than any other piece of the puzzle that, from a holistic perspective, is moving the planet toward a more peaceful, joyful, creative, diverse and well-integrated being. It is my job to do my pieces and do them well, and at the same time to fully support those who are doing other pieces. Ultimately, I entrust my fate to these other beings, knowing that this big puzzle does indeed fit together.

This is my definition of real community — people dedicated to being in Service to the planet, cross-fertilizing each other's creativity. I love the aspect of living together as well, and I think co-habitation (whether as neighbors or housemates) amps up the wattage on our support capacity with each other; but it's not necessary. What is necessary is that we encourage each other, celebrate each other's wins as our wins, and simply act as companions along the way. I see it as important to honor each other because the people around me are doing many of the pieces that I don't personally have the time or inclination to do.

We need each other, because our collective creativity and passion is what is required to transform a planet. We can see needing each other as a big drag, an obligation or a guilt trip. This attitude breeds resentment and competition between natural allies because not everyone is as invested in our particular passion as we are. The alternative is that we can hold it as a joyful celebration and appreciate having aligned companions on a big, long, interesting journey, and see our differences as our strengths.

When we surround ourselves with people who understand our passions, our fears, our goals and our challenges, and are of the mind that we are in this together and are here to help, then we have an easier time persevering. Have you ever tried to move ahead in your life surrounded by people who just don't get it? Who don't even get why you'd want to move ahead? It's like swimming upstream — you can do it, but the extra effort it takes drains you, slows you down, and generally just makes things difficult.

It is essential that we interact in the world with people we disagree with. However, we are most likely to be successful when we have a supportive network of people to help us stay focused, relaxed and recharged, and occasionally nurse our wounds. This support is essential for most of us to do the work we need to do on behalf of the planet and our own health, happiness and wholeness. Work on tough issues, expose yourself to people in a different place (emotionally and mentally) don't avoid these bigger challenges... but do it with a knowledge that when you go home at night, or get to the weekend, you'll be embraced by people who love life with the same vigor you do, to whom you don't need to explain your joy, and with whom you can just be.

Create a community for yourself of aligned beings, and you can do anything.

And for those who are ready for a really full exploration of community, there is the Intentional Communities (IC) Movement, and the possibility of living with a group of people. There are ICs all over the planet, and they come in all sizes, focuses, levels of intensity, etc.[47] I have lived for 12 years now in intentional, residential communities—one that could have passed in many ways for a

---

[47] From the *Communities Directory*: "An 'intentional community' is a group of people who have chosen to live or work together in pursuit of a common ideal or vision. Most, though not all, share land or housing. Intentional communities come in all shapes and sizes, and display an amazing diversity in their common values, which may be social, economic, spiritual, political and/or ecological. Some are rural; some urban. Some live all in a single residence; some in separate households. Some raise children; some don't. Some are secular, some are spiritually based, and others are both. For all their variety though, the communities featured (here) hold a common commitment to living cooperatively, to solving problems non-violently, and to sharing their experiences with others." The *Communities Directory* is published by and available through the Fellowship for Intentional Community, www.ic.org.

stereotypical income sharing "60's commune"; one a small, just starting spiritual community; one an urban co-op house; and one a rural ecovillage. And right now, I am writing from my living room in a desert, urban "ecohood."

Some ICs support work on a particular political issue. Others are just about sharing resources and knowing your neighbors, and some are tied to a particular religious doctrine or spiritual practice. All provide the opportunity for personal growth, closeness and experimental living.

And while some operate with a hierarchical, dictatorial sort of decision-making, the vast majority (and those that I have found to be really gratifying to be a part of) operate with a more truly democratic and human-scale decision-making than we get in our version of democracy, often with consensus, which stretches us all to be in tune with what is best for a whole group of people. For those of us involved in sustainability work, striving to understand how to be in our lives in a way that fully accounts for the well being of a whole planet, living in community can be a great fit.

Living more communally is also almost automatically more ecologically sound than living in separate households. This is true even in those communities who really have no intention of being a sustainable living project. Mostly, this is because every community I have seen does at least some minimal resource sharing (i.e. they own one lawn mower for 30 people, instead of 10 of them) and at least some of your social life is right there, within walking distance.

Most IC's go well beyond that. They share meals, which

177

means less human and physical resources are being used to prepare and clean up from them. Some share vehicles, cutting down considerably on the number of cars needed. Most have some common facilities, including laundry and guest spaces, which eliminates the need for every household to be big enough to accommodate these things (and as a result, drops the square footage that each household is heating, cooling and otherwise maintaining.)

Some even have "luxury" items like a hot tub and extensive playground facilities, which most people can't afford on our own. One of the really great things about living in community is that we can have a higher "standard of living" with less income[48]. That translates into more free time to pursue what matters, and less pressure for people wanting to move toward right livelihood.

Living in community is not Utopian. There are real and sometimes painful challenges. But these challenges are... well, *real*... I believe that living in community gives you the opportunity to roll up your sleeves and be part of figuring out how the heck to get along

---

[48] In some communities, this is very dramatic. I was a member for 2 1/2 years of East Wind Community in rural Missouri. At the time, East Wind had roughly 70 people who got by with 7 cars and two laundry machines. We had guest spaces, music space, hundreds of acres of land, huge organic gardens and ranch, playgrounds, a low-tech hot tub, and retreat space. The "work week" was 40 hours, but included childcare and home schooling time, cooking, some cleaning and laundry work, gardening, etc—many of the things usually considered "domestic work." In exchange for your 40 hours, you got food, shelter (not fancy, but adequate) health care, childcare, fresh air, varied work, and a small monthly stipend for whatever else you wanted. For those for whom the social scene works, it's a pretty good deal. While the social scene ultimately wasn't right for my family, I have tremendous respect for the financial and labor experiment that East Wind and other egalitarian, income-sharing communities are engaged in. You can find East Wind and over a thousand other communities listed directory.ic.org.

with people (which contributes to world peace) and how to be on the planet in a more gentle way (which contributes to world livability).

Chapter 13: With One Foot in Creative Possibility

"Political and personal hopes are intertwined, of course. What keeps us committed to improving our communities and our country is akin to what gives us strength to endure the sometimes devastating difficulties of our individual lives."

--From the introduction to *The Impossible Will Take a Little While*, edited by Paul Rogat Loeb

The root words for our modern word attention are from Latin, and they translate as "stretch toward." To put your attention on something is quite literally to stretch yourself toward it. When you place your attention, you get closer to the thing you are attending to[49].

Is your attention on the earth's health and beauty, or is it on pollution and the ugliness? Put another way, do you label yourself an optimist or a pessimist? In reality, there is no such thing as "an

---

[49] I was introduced to this way of viewing attention through my Avatar work.

optimist" or "a pessimist" — there is optimism and pessimism; to label ourselves permanently one or the other is to fix ourselves in a reality that doesn't serve anyone. But certainly most people lean more in one direction or the other.

Optimism heals; pessimism picks apart and destroys.

What does it mean to be in a state of optimism? (I'm going to use the term "in" to describe this, because optimism and pessimism are both states of mind, states of being, a psychic "space" we put ourselves in, by choice or default.) In optimism, the details of life around you are wondrous at best, and interesting at the least. The big picture is big enough to encompass a future different than the one that may be more obviously unfolding in front of you. Optimism is the place of possibility, of openness, of hope. Optimism is a roomy thing.

In pessimism, the details are ugly and we find ourselves inexplicably drawn to what's wrong. The big picture feels bigger than us, and it is overwhelming. We feel small, and crowded by the problems. Pessimism is the psychic equivalent of an untouched closet. It is the perspective of a status quo trying to preserve itself, at any cost.

Pessimism can be easy to maintain, but there's no payoff. Because it requires no imagination, it embodies no real creative potential. Cultivate pessimism within yourself, and you are cultivating your own dead end.

Optimism, on the other hand, can be challenging to maintain, not because it is any more or less true than pessimism (none of this discussion is really about some immutable "truth") or because it doesn't see clearly, but precisely because it requires of us a leap of faith, outside of the box, whatever box we have created for ourselves. But within optimism, there is the seed of payoffs—huge payoffs. Imagination opens possibilities to create a different life, a different set of relationships, and a different planet. Optimism is the perspective of cultural evolution. It is the perspective of embodied Spirit, of a living, vibrant God if you will.

Optimism is not a refusal to see what is there—that is denial (which, oddly enough, is more like pessimism in that it is also easy, and also has no payoff potential.) Optimism is the willingness to see exactly what is there, through the eyes of hope and creative possibility. Professional problem solvers, the really good ones, are essentially professionals at optimism. It is what I experienced in India time and time again—people living their lives with presence, without resistance and within a "can do" frame of mind.

Real optimism sees clearly, and decides to apply the best of one's internal potential to an outside situation. It is internally generated hope holding space for things to change. Optimism applied opens the door for real communion; there is no space for real connection and deep creative bonding in the presence of pessimism. You may bond within pessimism, as your cynicism finds agreement, but it is a bonding within safe, fixed parameters of limitation, and therefore, it will never take you beyond what you are seeing at that moment (which likely isn't much fun, and isn't very productive) because real communion comes with the risk of hope.

We are not optimists and pessimists (the old "there are two types of people in the world" jokes aside.) All of us slip into pessimism at times, and all of us have flashes of optimism. Clinging to easy labels is part of the pessimism of the world—holding easy, non-creative limitations on ourselves or others is part of how we hold ourselves and each other back and disempowered, and it is a form of denial to label someone in a fixed way and refuse to see them as a whole person. It is true that some people choose to spend more time in one state of mind or the other, but the truth is, we are all tempted by the ease and safety of pessimism, and we are all a bit intimidated by the vigilance it takes to stay optimistic in the world.

There is nothing more important to the planet at this time than cultivating the clear-seeing, creative, open space of optimism and then acting on it. Optimism gives more energy than it takes, and it is the source of real hope in the world. The amazing, creative architect William McDonough was once asked in an interview in *Yes!* magazine if he really thought his work could change the world, and he essentially said, "I don't know, but I am going to try." That's optimism! No denial of the state of things, no need for easy answers, but a simple, hopeful, diligent movement forward.

Pessimism makes statistics and blame into the end game, because it cannot truly see and inspire anything beyond them. Pessimism is what insists that we debate facts endlessly, and that we can do nothing until we have all those facts lined up and categorized properly. It is truly nothing more than a game to keep ourselves in a state of non-creativity.

And why? Because creativity is hopeful and risky and we necessarily step outside of what we know and what we can explain in simple terms to the people around us. There is no logical, in-this-moment, satisfying and complete explanation for why one acts upon optimism, because optimism lives with only one foot in this moment—the other foot is stretching forward into the unknown and outside of our current reality.

This is faith, and you can't explain faith; but you also can't live a vibrant, creative life of contribution without it.

And that flatly runs counter to several foundations of modern American culture. We are obsessed, for instance, with insurance and security. We deny the very nature of life itself in this obsession, and we create endless stress and additional work for ourselves by it. The flourishing of the insurance industry is one of the most obvious signs that we are out of touch with our own creativity. The more we buy in to the "need" for insuring everything, the more we remove ourselves from the moment. Like many perceived "needs," the desire to have every important possession insured is actually a cultural crutch. Real needs (the basics that Henry David Thoreau detailed over a hundred years ago—food, shelter, warmth in the winter and cool in the summer—those types of needs) get lost in the shuffle of shopping lists for security and status.

Our obsession with insurance is a type of structural pessimism; it keeps us in a box of concern, anxiety and fears, and denies more creative solutions to our challenges. We Americans have a myth about ourselves that says that we are all about creativity; in

185

reality, we play things pretty safe.

So what does this have to do with activism? Simply this — we are living, and doing our activism work, within a culture that is fundamentally biased toward pessimistic, safe approaches to some very basic questions: What do we define as needs? How do we meet these needs? What is worth protecting? What is the relationship between comfort and security? Between money and needs?

All of these questions, and their answers, color the lenses of our lives at a very basic level, and our activism is not separate from our lives. If we base our daily lives on assumptions that are fundamentally pessimistic, pessimism will flourish. If we base our daily lives on assumptions that are fundamentally optimistic, optimism will flourish.

So in shifting your attention from the pessimistic to the optimistic, be prepared to run into some very fundamental questions about how you structure your life, about what's really important, about who you really are. And be prepared, as you become more creative, to not always have a logical reason for doing what you are doing that the people around you can easily understand. When you put one foot into creative possibility, you stretch outside of the current moment, the current culture and the current paradigm with all its assumptions.

Optimism is a radical act that spins together the best of love and hope, and paves the way to prosperity, ease and beauty. But be prepared for a leap of faith.

Pessimism vacillates wildly between feeling stuck on the one hand and demanding a revolution at any cost on the other. Both extremes are equally wedded to hopelessness. We can wait for the revolution, and use that as an excuse to not just buckle down and get on with changing ourselves, and our own communities. Waiting on a revolution is the best excuse we could possibly manufacture for not being responsible here and now. Revolution is a myth—if we force change via violence, we've simply bought into violence in a different way. Unless we cultivate within ourselves a different structure of power and integrity, there will be no one prepared to run the post-revolution world any differently than that which we are looking to overturn. The faces may change, but without evolution of consciousness, the game will be the same.

Optimism, on the other hand, is *evolutionary*—steady, diligent and hopeful. There is no need for violence in order to change; there is simply being and doing the change. Beyond revolutionary politics is the simple and radical belief that humans are fundamentally good, and we can trust each other. At the heart of optimism is a deep faith in humanity. And because we all have proof abundant for how humans can be cruel (perhaps, in our most honest moments, seeing that proof even in our own behavior) taking that leap of faith in our fellow humans is scary as hell. But it is this faith itself, this appreciation for the journey and willingness to show up and support each other on the path, that creates the environment in which this faith will be repaid by our best and brightest acts.

One of the truisms of humanity is that we rise to a challenge. You can see this most easily with kids—one parent expects them to cooperate, and they do; another expects a fight, and they get it. Is your idea of humanity one that is challenging the people around you — and yourself — to rise to an optimistic challenge? Or a pessimistic one? If people truly acted just as you expect them to, would the world be a better place for your input, or a worse place?

You cannot separate your own consciousness from how the people around you behave. This is one of the links between personal responsibility and the delicately linked world of community and mass consciousness. But to be an activist is to accept responsibility for something larger than yourself, and at its roots being an activist is a noble and wonderful thing. And how you envision people is as important as any phone calls you make or things you buy or don't buy.

It is the foundation upon which your own effectiveness rests.

To go into an interaction assuming that the people around you don't care and won't hear it is to set yourself up to not be heard. If the goal for having that conversation is one that serves the planet, then your failure is not only personal, but also affects the planet. To go into an interaction with a commitment to hear and be heard, to share and to be enlightened by the people you are sharing with, is to set yourself up to succeed and make a real impact on the lives of the people you interact with, and in turn to have that positive impact on the planet itself. When you expect to be heard, you act in accordance with that expectation and show a patient willingness to engage that makes it far more likely to manifest as a reality.

When I talk about viewing the earth as a limited being and a

188

restriction, I am essentially talking about occupying the planet in a state of continuous pessimism. When I talk about viewing the earth as an opportunity, I am talking about embodying optimism as our main filter for interacting with the planet. The former will eventually kill us; the latter is a path to an enlightened, abundant future.

Examples of optimistic attitudes:

- We'll create a solution that will work for everyone.
- I can do this.
- If I pursue right livelihood, I'll be cared for.
- The world is essentially a friendly placed.
- I can trust myself.
- The world is headed in a positive, evolutionary direction.
- Humanity is creative.
- Living on the planet is an opportunity to create great things.

Chapter 14: Passion as Big as a Planet

Optimism alone won't change the world; it is simply the attitude in consciousness that opens the door for it and holds the space. Combined with passionate action though, it suddenly becomes an effective tool. Passion is one of the more misunderstood concepts of our time, and it is, hands down, the most important legacy I inherited from my father's family.

Passion is not anger, or intensity of emotion. It is not drama. Real passion, in fact, is rarely loud at all.

Passion is a quiet, steady excitement that motivates positive action, keeps us going, and brings a sparkle into our lives and everything we do. Passion is based in a deep valuing of the thing or person your passion is directed toward—passion is, in short, an energized, connected reverence put into action.

You can be passionate about a lover, or your children. You can be passionate about a project, an organization or business, a line of work, a particular writer's work or type of music. Passion of the highest type draws us toward enlightenment, deeper connection with others and our own life purpose. It is always aligned with an internal sense of something being right for you, and it engenders wonder and fascination with all things connected to it.

Passion can be infectious, and sometimes one person's passion can help us overcome our prejudices. I have a friend named Jonathan Wolfe who became interested in fractals (those patterns in the natural world that repeat themselves, and fold back on themselves with larger units of a pattern being made up of smaller units of that same pattern) while getting a PhD in neuroscience. Jonathan has taken on the mission of inspiring children's interest in math (which, despite what my son tells me, generally strikes me as one of the three most boring topics in the universe) by using the beauty of fractals. We spent two hours one night watching Jonathan's slide presentation about fractals, and by the end of it, I *wanted* to understand the math.

His joy in sharing a sincerely held passion was contagious. And because I allowed myself to be "infected," I am now much more willing to see the value in his work and the work of others in his field, with sincerity and even moments of fascination. Jonathan's passion creates a bridge between people[50].

Passion lets us go places that are true growth edges, because passion for any topic held sincerely enough will tug on the strings of everything else. It doesn't actually matter where we start in life. If you pursue something for long enough and with a sincere enough effort, it will wind you through every area of life, because everything is connected.

My own path has been about as winding as it gets. I started out in environmental activism, explored paganism and feminism, got a gender studies degree, did gay and racial equity activism, worked for a co-op, explored consciousness, landed in intentional community, got interested in ecovillages... and found myself right back where I started, as an eco-activist. In a world of optimism and passionate engagement, everything you bump into is fair game for exploration, because you relate it all back to your passion.

And it isn't even so much about what we are actually doing with our time. It is often simply an ability to let one's mind and heart roam and find the connections between things. Explore the business world for long enough, and eventually you'll be part of looking at ethics, or space design, or group empowerment issues. Explore personal growth for long enough, and eventually you'll deal with money issues, or politics, or how your personal actions affect the planet. Tug on any strand of this tapestry called life, and eventually the whole cloth unfolds.

Passion should never be judged. I have recently gotten to be close to a man who is a quintessential geek. What I am learning from him is that "geekdom" is essentially the ability to get passionately wrapped up in things that most people around you could care less about. Through his eyes, I have gained a deeper appreciation for the ability to get intensely excited about things, and the brilliance that

---

[50] To find out more about Jonathan's work, check out www.fractalfoundation.org

comes from doing so about a wide range of topics and then being able to spin it all together to get a truly holistic understanding of life in general. He has a different set of knowledge than I do: permaculture, computers, landscaping, Southwest cultural history... When you put them all together, he's one of the most brilliant people I've ever met when it comes to systems thinking, because he's played with it from so many different angles. I'm in awe of how his mind works, even though some of his areas (like computers) don't hold a lot of personal interest for me.

So, passion should never be judged. Be passionate about your piece of the puzzle, and find the connections as your path leads you through them. The biggest mistake we can make is to work on our piece and discount the value of other pieces, even those pieces that we see no immediate value in. In ten years, you'll be a wiser person, with more experience in the world, and then you may see the connection you don't see now. Even without understanding the value of something, our support (or at least our willingness to withhold disparagement) can help a field move forward in a positive direction, and who knows what the benefits of your support will be?

For years, economics was just a class I had hated in college, and a bunch of moneygrubbers on Wall Street who could care less. I judged people who went into the field as having their priorities all wrong. But in recent years, the work of local currency activists, folks involved in socially responsible investment funds, and alternative credit unions has begun to turn my head. I've started to pay more attention to this realm of life. Suddenly I wish I hadn't dismissed economics so thoroughly. I find myself wondering if my disparagement made a negative impact; and how my willingness to give it a fair shake could have made a positive one. First, I wouldn't have wasted my energy being critical and my own work could be further along. Second, perhaps our two fields would be even closer together, more harmoniously linked if I (and people like me) had been open to stretching to see the value in their work. Perhaps they would have been more willing all along to stretch to see the value in mine.

Of course, part of why any field goes astray and gets mired in stuff that isn't positive for the world is that lots of people aren't following their passion, and for them, their work is just work. They haven't found that internal alignment with the higher good. You can find that in any field, and you can contribute some wonderful piece in any field, but in order to find your niche, you need to be willing to trust yourself. Whatever your real passion is, the earth will benefit from you finding it and pursuing it, even if you can't see how that is right now.

As people become more tuned into their right livelihood and right actions (and by "right" actions I mean right in a way that is aligned with your own intuition; I don't mean some theoretical ethical standard, nor do I mean some absolute) we will naturally become more responsible. And that can only be of benefit to the earth in the long run.

Passion is a combination of focus, intent, excitement and presence. When we say we are passionate about something, we usually mean that we will extend ourselves beyond our own needs and desires

195

on its behalf and put in some real time and energy for it—it means we will go out of our way for it, love it, nurture it and be joyful in its presence. To be passionate about a lover, or a project or a planet is to awaken a sense of valuing and excitement about it, and step into creative risk taking.

Passion is what draws us out of ourselves and into real engagement in the world. The planet and its people will survive and flourish to the degree that we get passionate about it and start acting on its behalf.

Chapter 15: Faith and Hope for the 21st Century

"Hope is believing in spite of the evidence, then watching the evidence change."

—Jim Wallis, editor of *Sojourners* magazine

We must return to—or perhaps more truthfully for many of us, create from whole cloth—a real faith in humanity.

Intelligence is often seen in the environmental movement as something that can provide technical fixes, but not honored as something that could provide sane decisions to simply stop creating those problems that we spend so much energy addressing. Voluntary simplicity—a concept articulated so lovingly by Duane Elgin 30-some years ago—is a much less frequent part of the discussion than hydrogen cells and disposal technology.

Without a simple faith in simple human ethics and

intelligence, I believe we are lost.

There is nothing wrong with seeking technological responses to problems. Nor am I, obviously, suggesting that we abandon activism. Quite the opposite; I believe that actions and solutions of all sorts are necessary when dealing with complex problems.

I am suggesting, however, that *how* we do this work matters tremendously. If we do it out of limitation, fear and an attempt to save something, that is coming out of a profoundly flawed and co-dependent place: you don't go into a relationship trying to fix the other party and expect to have it be a healthy, nurturing relationship. When we see the earth as a partner, we need to apply those lessons learned in our years of human relationship work and change the focus to co-creative efforts that are inspiring and are deeply in Service to both parties. (The earth is, of course, already doing its part in Service to us, in the form of food, water, air, beauty, etc. We've just been missing the boat on our part of the deal.)

It is also key that we make this change, because we are doing an awfully effective job of turning off those people who are in a position to contribute the most to the movement—those who have reached a personal state of real health and joy, and who have a capacity to create life-beyond-fear. Without powerful, healthy allies, the movement is floundering. We are losing some of the best and the brightest thinkers and doers to those fields that are most profoundly about supporting emotional and spiritual health—including the personal growth movements, and natural healing.

People who are ready to let go of limitation thinking, the

blame game and pessimism, find themselves drawn to and most easily supported in those movements that operate from a new paradigm. Those are the people we want in the movement; those are the people that it is worth changing our general vibe in order to attract.

So, we have a whole swath of incredibly healthy, productive, joyful people, a lot of whom are now former activists, and have decided that the best place to put their energy is in the domain of creating preferred personal realities. Why? Because the ecological movement (and I'd venture a guess that this is true of other social movements as well) hasn't kept up with the personal and spiritual growth movements in the areas of personal responsibility, compassion and cooperation. For the most part, we are still deeply invested in blame and competition, and it is frankly unappealing.

To quote a favorite 8-year-old: it feels yucky.

But here's the thing: once you achieve the capacity to create your own personal goals and have reached a stable place of happiness (which is happening in the personal growth field) you start looking for bigger goals. It becomes very attractive and even compelling to be deeply in Service to others and to the planet, and to create something of real value. Personal growth that is focused only on one's own needs and health stagnates after a while. Healthy, happy people want to be in Service to others, because it is the next natural step once you've achieved happiness for yourself to want to share it with others.

If we do not, as a movement, have a place for these people to contribute once they have explored the domain of personal goals to their satisfaction, where they are honored for their work, then we lose out. And we are losing out. The healthier I have gotten, the more tempting it has been to jump ship on the environmental movement. In truth, I've already jumped ship on many organizations within the movement for exactly these reasons.

So, what does it mean to have space in a movement for truly healthy people? I see the minimal requirements for attracting and keeping this new breed of activist to be the following:

- being open to real, transformational dialogue focused on creative possibility (instead of survival)
- a willingness to look at our own stuff instead of blaming others
- paying people well for their work (not doing so is a classic example of limitations thinking)
- and finally, a real, grounded hope and faith in the people around us, including those people across the table from us at negotiations and city council meetings.

While it is certainly true that the most committed people will work out of love, no matter what the circumstances, it is also true that the culture will be more vibrant and more appealing to a wider range of people if we can cultivate these values. Broader appeal ultimately means having an easier time with all of our work, because there are fewer people who see themselves as being outside of the movement.

It's really about revisioning the environmental activism movement as a supportive and nurturing community... that will eventually include most of the people the planet.

Chapter 16: Into the Journey: Some Advice for Companions

I offer the following three snippets for folks who are engaged in the practical work of inspiring others and teaching. Paying attention to them can help you be more effective.

#1: Grow at a Sustainable Rate of Change

I honestly believe that there is such a thing as a sustainable rate of change. When we are making changes, it is wise to plan for some integration time. By integration I mean the process of a change becoming the norm in your life—getting used to yourself in a new place, or getting used to a new routine or view on life. Something that is well integrated is easily accessible to you—you *think through* it, naturally, instead of having to deliberately put attention on it.

On very rare occasions, people can make massive radical life changes in a short period of time—an epiphany hits, and it is powerful enough to create its own momentum. More often than not, however, epiphanies start a process of introspection, and introspective action leads to a new *path or direction*.

Sometimes people get inspired to make changes in their lives, and the pressure of having recognized that something in their lives is not ideal pushes them to want to change everything right now. This isn't a path; it's more like a mid-life crisis. If you try to change everything all at once, what happens more often than not is that you get overwhelmed and give up. This is because you don't yet have the routines in place to support the new change, or the re-worked thinking to back it up. This can be disastrous, because you have now provided evidence for yourself that you can't do it, or it's not worth it, or it's really hard, etc. and the net result may be that you make very little or no progress at all.

This is one of the ways that a movement dies out—if there is a demand for people to change more quickly than they are able to integrate. This considerably undermines the effectiveness of the movement in two ways: 1) by creating a belief in the public consciousness that the work of the movement is difficult if not impossible; and 2) by unnecessarily slowing down people who do *have* the commitment to keep working through initial failure, but who waste their energy experiencing struggle instead of real, steady change.

The value of following a path is that you are able to make a change, integrate it and feel solid again. This achievement strengthens

204

you to then make another change. Why court struggle? Gradual change is ultimately faster than trying to rush things, and it keeps your peace of mind intact.

Of course the better your personal growth tools, and the more willingly you engage them, the more quick and effortless your version of "gradual" can be, while still maintaining a good sense of equilibrium and feeling integrated. I've seen people change major life patterns in a weekend, with good support, good willingness and good tools. I've also seen people struggle for endless periods with small stuff when those factors are missing. So as you are working toward change, pause and take stock, honestly, of how good your support, willingness and tools are.

Recognize, too, that big decisions and goals are important guideposts for your life, but they are essentially irrelevant if there is not a series of small daily decisions and steps in place that make up a changed life. You can have all the goals in the world. But if you are not willing to wake up in the morning and orient your daily life toward that goal, it will stay in the ethers. This means making those phone calls, saving that gallon of water, choosing to listen rather than engage in an angry outburst. Moment-to-moment decisions and action are the stuff of a good, aligned life.

Growth can be easy and joyful and fun. It doesn't have to be a struggle. Change can be easy and joyful and fun. It doesn't need to be painful.

The belief that growth and change are hard is a deeply damaging one because it slows people down. This slow down is one way we collectively build our body of evidence about how hard it is, and simultaneously provide a motivation for people to cling to the pretense of being somewhere that we aren't. We try to skip these growth steps, and then fail miserably, convincing ourselves in the process that it is hard. It *isn't* hard, so long as you accept where you are and go from there, taking only the step that is in front of you.

I'm not living a totally sustainable life. If I tried to claim that, I'd be operating from pretense, and something about my words just wouldn't ring true for people. I am a few steps further down the road than most Americans, and I am committed to continue on this path because it aligns with my internal sense of ethics. I'm able to facilitate people's growth effectively because I've been there, and I have some general sense of the path they'll take in their own journey. I'm a companion, and I have compassion for the stretch. When someone comes into my world who is further along than I am, I get to be in the student role. It's fun and interesting, and it always illuminates and inspires the next step or two.

If I suddenly tried to implement all the changes that would be required for me to live a fully sustainable life, I'd most likely experience pain, struggle and failure, because that is many steps down the road from where I am. So long as I continue a steady process of taking the next step... and then the next step... and then the next step... the process continues to unfold with joy, and I am able to sustain those changes without feeling overwhelmed and giving up on the whole thing.

So, while I am saying that I believe there is such a thing as a

206

sustainable rate of change, I also want to acknowledge that this may feel painfully slow to those who feel some understandable urgency about the state of the planet. The only real comfort I can offer is that I believe that honoring our own growth curves and taking our own self-determined next steps will get us there a lot more quickly than trying to force it beyond where we can maintain and build on the changes we are making. Remember the story about the Tortoise and the Hare?

This step-by-step approach is not subject to constant failure and restart, because those changes can integrate in as we go along. (And you know when something new has integrated because it has become comfortable and you no longer need to think about it, or expend lots of effort for it to happen.) Even if you do have an occasional failure along the way, if it really is just one step you are working on, the failure will be a small one; if you bite off a huge chunk all at once and fail at that, it's a much bigger deal. Better, by far, to do things in manageable pieces, and adopt a steady approach. In five years, you will be much further along adopting this method than trying to do everything perfectly all at once.

The other advantage to this approach is that self-responsibility builds personal power. When you are more responsible for your own life, you are less subject to being thrown off-kilter or to being unsure of yourself in the face of other powerful people. You are more able to listen and less likely to react, because it doesn't matter so much what the other person is saying or doing. You are clear that you are able to be secure and responsible because you've built that confidence up

207

over a period of time.

Once you have built up sufficient personal power, you could sit in the board room and talk to a company head, without feeling threatened or needing to make them wrong for their perspective. And that's a lot more powerful than yelling from the sidewalk, because you are able to meet them where they are at, on their own turf, and hold your own. There are no sore spots of self-doubt to be pushed on; you are equals in dialogue. Instead of petitioner to power, you are power to power.

You may, perhaps, even learn something valuable to you by being able to meet other powerful beings at their level. From this place, exchange can happen, and new possibilities can unfold that might meet everyone's needs even better than what we imagined on our own—co-creation instead of competition of perspectives.

A couple years ago, I got to work with an organization that supports the development of small businesses, offering loans, classes and technical support to women entrepreneurs. The woman we worked with was, in 1997, a successful player on Wall Street. Five years ago, I would have been incredibly intimidated by this woman, who is powerful, experienced and competent in worlds that I've never even seen. But we were able to sit together in creative partnership, and my ease with myself translated into an ease with her, in spite of my feeling very out of place in the business world. Coming from seemingly opposite worlds, we were able to meet in the middle, and learned from each other in the process.

#2: The Ability of the Human Mind to Grok Your Message

There's an odd phenomenon that activists ought to be aware of: people can only take in thoughts, concepts, facts and occurrences that fit within *the size* of their framework. Make something too small, and it won't be worth their attention; make something too big, and it simply can't be taken in and accepted. Huge disasters, like the tsunami at the end of 2004, cannot really be comprehended by people; even sitting within it, those people who have been forced to deal with it directly, losing loved ones and their livelihood, go numb, and only take in a certain amount of what is happening at any given time.

The size of someone's comprehensibility is often a very literal thing. Give someone a fact that fits a reference point that is familiar enough to them, and suddenly something that has been too big for them, or too distant, will take on a reality for them that allows them then to act. For me, the size of my reference point that got me motivated around rainforest activism was a football field.

I don't remember the exact statistic. But I do know that I had been hearing bits and pieces for several years about rainforest destruction, about how much was being lost and the horrible impact that was having on our world. Sometimes it seemed so small—a kind of plant was lost. And most of the time it was so huge that I just never quite wrapped my head around it. And then someone had the wherewithal to put it into a measurement I could understand: a football field. It was some amount of time in which it took to lose a football field's worth of rain forest—a half hour maybe? I can't

209

remember the specifics now, but I do know that suddenly, for a girl who had literally grown up going to the "Big House" (the football stadium at the University of Michigan) every year of my life, I could SEE what they were saying, and suddenly I was personally horrified by the scale of the destruction.

As intellectually sympathetic as I'd been about rainforest preservation, I had never been able to get passionate about it until that moment. It seems ridiculous—the statistic hadn't changed, the reality in Brazil hadn't changed, my basic sensibilities hadn't changed. All that had changed was that I found a way to visualize it that hit home.

There is a term in the study of literature called defamiliarization. It is taking something so familiar that we don't even see it any more and presenting a perspective on it that allows the reader to see it anew. It's like that moment when you are driving the same route to work you've taken every day for years, and suddenly, there's a "new" hotel there that you never noticed before (never mind that it's as old as you are...) You have that momentary shock of recognition that something seems to have changed while you weren't looking. In reality all that's changed is your consciousness—you just became aware of something you'd been ignoring or not seeing for years.

Finding a reference point that hits home is a form of defamiliarization, and it is something that we desperately need. We need to see with fresh eyes—personal eyes—the challenges in front of us. But for those of us who have grown up with factories all around and cars and the slow spread of our cities, it has become so familiar that we don't register the small encroaching of hopelessness and erosion of life around us.

It isn't about guilt-tripping people in a new and interesting way designed to shock; that's not what I am suggesting, and it is a method that's been tried and seems to result in at least as much alienation from the movement as it leads to inspiration. It's about finding that *personal connection* that will allow each of us to see our lives—and the impact of our lives—more and more clearly, and not flinch away or go numb in the face of the challenge of personal responsibility. It requires that our activism become closer to home as well, personal enough that we can connect the message in a meaningful way to different people. And we'll only know how to connect if we take the time to get to know the person.

Here's a general rule to invoke when considering the value of any given "message" and how to communicate it: Defamiliarization with heartlessness leads to anger; defamiliarization with compassion and enrollment leads to commitment.

#3: Knowing When to Share Increases your Effectiveness

It's sometimes a little tricky to know when it will be useful to share information or make suggestions. I have three questions I ask myself in those moments:

1) Is this person interested and open to hearing it?

2) Is this person more likely to use the information in a compassionate way, or more likely to beat up on themselves or others with it?

3) Am I in a good place to share the information, or will I be guilt tripping or otherwise less than human and understanding about where they are at?

If a person isn't open, it's a waste of everyone's time to try. If the person is likely to use the information in a counterproductive way, my goal of being in Service to the planet will be contradicted. And finally, if I can't be compassionate, then the interaction is likely to fail. If any one of the three is missing, with rare exception, I take the approach of silently appreciating the person and holding my tongue.

Finally, I trust my body and my intuition. If it doesn't feel right to bring something up, I don't. Connecting more deeply with the earth, respecting its inherent wisdom, is a valuable thing to do, and we can practice that by learning to listen to our own bodies.

I have one exception to this three-part rule, and this seems like the best ending for the book I can imagine. If someone in your circle has decided to take on a leadership role, speak up.

I was recently out working with two friends when an opportunity to give someone some feedback presented itself. This man has been in my circle for several years and I have always really liked him. He took a sort of social hiatus for a while, and when he came back out of his own contemplation, he was on fire about starting a new project. The project is great, and he is doing the brave work of stepping into the unfamiliar territory of leadership in order to make it happen.

The hard part for me is that he's also come out of his contemplations full of "piss and vinegar" as my grandmother used to say. The good news is, he now has a fire in him that is motivating him to act; the bad news is, he's not interested in working with certain groups of people because he sees them as contributing to what's wrong with the world. As I listened to him speak, I thought that, while there is some definite truth in his assessment, there are also plenty of people who self-identify in these groups are who actually doing good work.

If I had stuck rigidly with my own criteria for giving feedback, I wouldn't have said anything: I wasn't clear if he was open to the feedback, I didn't know for sure what he'd do with it, and his energy was strong enough that I was getting a little triggered myself. But I was also clear that stepping into leadership means you are going to get the feedback in some way or another—either someone will tell you gently, someone will tell you harshly or, worse, no one will tell you at all and your project will just flounder. I figured I was in good enough shape to be the gentle version.

So I took a deep breath and laid it out as best I could, with one of those internal, "Here we go…" feelings. At first, I wasn't sure if I had made the right call. But then he asked me, "Am I putting people off?" and I answered as honestly as I could—not yet, but you could.

213

He came back to me twenty minutes later and said thank you, with a thoughtful look on his face, and a genuine hug. When presented with a chance for self-reflection, he took it, and that's a great sign. If I hadn't spoken, I probably would have walked away feeling distanced from him, like I had let him down by being afraid of his response. What I got instead was confirmation of an earlier assessment I had made: He's a really good man, and he is growing into his leadership just fine.

It doesn't always go well, but more and more it seems to be. And so I'm dedicated to keeping on with it. I'll see you on the journey.

Chapter 17: Enlightened Eco-Activism in a Nutshell

- Good activism begins with personal responsibility. Model it in your own life to learn how to actually do it. This creates honesty and resonance when we speak.
- Cultivate compassion, and your world will change. Create real support for others to be honest, responsible and kind.
- Stay dedicated to the planet, like a lifelong lover.
- The most direct way to care for the planet is to focus on your bioregion. Buy local, work local, love local, use local currencies.
- Work toward partnership, and away from demands that polarize.
- Replace laws with ethics.
- Listen more than you speak; act more than you lobby.
- Start with your personal domain and move outward from there.
- Adopt an attitude of consensus; listen for agreement, be curious, honor the variety of perspectives that any given topic will evoke.
- Voluntary simplicity means less stuff, less hours of work to support your stuff, more human connection and quality time.

- Create community in place of isolation. Live in community, shop at co-ops, develop car and biodiesel co-ops, get to know your neighbors.
- Right livelihood eliminates a whole range of justifications for acting unethically, improves your happiness, and shifts our culture toward money being a tool for good works.
- Keep moving ahead, but do it at a pace that feels empowering and not stressful.
- Enjoy the hell out of this beautiful planet and your opportunity to be here, now, in a body.

Appendix I: Resources

Personal Growth Tools:

- **Avatar:** The website for information on Avatar is: www.avatarepc.com For the best personal growth course I know, or to get Harry Palmer's books go to: www.avatarepc.com/html/bookstore.html

- **Non-Violent Communication:** communication that is about listening, clarity and respecting the other person. www.cnvc.org

- **Byron Katie's The Work,** recommended by numerous close friends as a simple approach to growth. /www.thework.com/

- *Power -vs- Force,* by Dr. David R. Hawkins. This book was used for a kinesiology experiment we did with Passion... and it is a fascinating read about the development of human consciousness.

- **Consensus and group process resources.** In addition to my own website (www.SolSpace.net) you can find information and training opportunities through:
  Laird Schaub, CANBRIDGE Consulting (nationwide) http://sandhillfarm.org/canbridge.html, and Tree Bressen and Caroline Estes (both on the West Coast) www.**treegroup**.info and www.casco.net/~alpha

Community Resources:

- **Fellowship for Intentional Community** is an the umbrella organization for all types of Intentional Communities, with a recent shift to include "Creating Community Where You Are" for those who want more community but aren't interested in formal IC living. www.ic.org. The FIC is essentially an information clearinghouse, without advocating for any particular model of community-building. Also available at this website:
  - *The Communities Directory*: listing over a thousand intentional communities, with maps, charts of information and community descriptions, plus a few articles. The FIC has both a print version and an on-line version of the directory.
  - *Communities: Life in Cooperative Culture*, a fabulous magazine for people who long for more community and connection in their lives.
  - *Visions of Utopia*: video documentary of communal history and modern examples of the varied ways to do it.

- **Federation of Egalitarian Communities**, for income-sharing, democratically run communities like the one I describe in the Context and Community chapter. www.thefec.org

- **Cohousing US** for one of the fastest growing versions of intentional community in the US, with more emphasis on private space, the Danish-inspired Cohousing model. www.cohousing.org

- **Global Ecovillage Network**: http://gen.ecovillage.org/ For information about communities with a focus on sustainability and sustainable development education.

Living Lightly Resources:

- *Voluntary Simplicity*, book by Duane Elgin. www.awakeningearth.org/ The concept of voluntary simplicity has been a formative one for me.

- **Habitat for Humanity,** www.habitat.org Creating partnerships with low income families for home ownership.

Printed in the United States
117026LV00006B/352/P